The
Complete Book
of

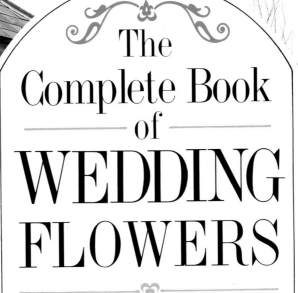

The
Complete Book
of
WEDDING
FLOWERS

Shirley Monckton

A CASSELL BOOK

First published in the UK
1993 by Cassell
Wellington House
125 Strand
London
WC2R 0BB

Reprinted 1993, 1994,

This edition 1995, reprinted 1998 twice, 1999

British Library Cataloguing-in-Publication Data
A catalogue record for this book is available from
the British Library

ISBN 0-304-34565-2

Typeset by Columns of Reading Ltd

Printed in China

PREVIOUS PAGES
*The garlands have been wired to the railings and
paper ribbon bows have been added. (Paper ribbon
lasts well in wet weather.) Berries, pods and green
spray carnations have been included with the various
foliages.*

*The pony and trap wait patiently for the bride and
her father. The back of the trap has been decorated
using simple wire-netting cages with floral foam to
take the flowers and foliages. The materials must be
placed firmly into the design to prevent them being
dislodged with the movement of the pony and trap.*

*Two obelisks that have been decorated with paper
ribbon bows stand smartly to attention on either side
of the door.*

CONTENTS

Acknowledgements

Writing, illustrating and designing the flower arrangements for this book have been great pleasures. However, without the willing and hard-working team of flower-arranging friends who so patiently and faithfully helped to interpret the ideas, they would have been impossible to accomplish. I wish to thank them for so many happy and very busy days of arranging flowers for The Complete Book of Wedding Flowers.

FLORISTRY AND FLOWER ARRANGING
  Barbara Mallard

FLOWER ARRANGING
  Brenda Akers, Trudy Blagrove, Iris Corrall, Gillian Evans, Margaret Smith

I also wish to thank the following for their help and kindness in allowing the use of their homes and churches, and in providing assistance in so many ways:

Mr and Mrs Guy Hart-Dyke, Lullingstone Castle, Eynsford.

The Reverend David Springthorpe, St Botolph's, Lullingstone, and St Martin's, Eynsford.

The Reverend John Lawrence, St Thomas More, West Malling.

The Reverend Brian Stevenson, St Mary the Virgin, West Malling.

Anashka, West Malling, bonnet and muff.

Tiers, West Malling, wedding cakes.

The Forge, Birling, wrought-iron containers.

Mid-Kent Cleaners, West Malling, linen.

Jean Graham, All Seasons, West Malling, flowers.

Mr Hood, Maidstone, marquee.

Mrs Breaker, Bayford Court Farm, Sittingbourne, pony and trap.

Both the photographer, Mike Evans, and the designer, Richard Carr, who were such a pleasure to work with.

And last but in no way the least, thanks to the husbands of all those who worked on the flowers, especially my own, who uncomplainingly supported the project.

INTRODUCTION

A thing of beauty is a joy for ever:
Its loveliness increases; it will never
Pass into nothingness; but still will keep
A bower quiet for us, and a sleep
Full of sweet dreams, and health,
          and quiet breathing.
                    John Keats, Endymion (1818)

THIS POIGNANT POEM describes exactly how I feel about flowers for weddings. It is of course true that the flowers so lovingly and beautifully arranged do fade and die, but they certainly never pass into 'nothingness'; they are for ever cherished memories.

A wedding is a joyous occasion, a time to celebrate, and flowers are a particularly lovely way to help create a beautiful setting for the perfect day.

In the following pages I have tried to show my delight in wedding designs and to illustrate how they can be arranged, with suggestions for alternative styles. No two occasions are ever the same, and this for me is so much a part of the excitement and the enjoyment. Ideas and plans are needed to create beautiful settings and, hopefully, the arrangements and illustrations in *The Complete Book of Wedding Flowers* will help to make that very special day unforgettable.

1

WEDDING FLOWER PLANS

THE ENGAGEMENT OF THE HAPPY COUPLE has been announced and it is now planning time in earnest for the wedding day. It always makes good sense to get on with the main plans as soon as the date has been decided; the church, the reception venue and all those who are to be involved will need ample time to get things prepared. It is also a relief to have all the major decisions made and settled, so that there is time to sit back and enjoy the engagement period, and be able to attend to all the details that will make the wedding a very special event rather than 'just another wedding'.

The decision about the place of marriage is a very personal one, and this of course is the first point from which to work. Once decided, and if a church has been chosen, it is advisable to book such other things as the choir and the bells, or whatever else will be required, at the same time. The next part of the plan must be the venue for the reception. It really is good thinking to have the reception within easy reach of the church, but if this is just not possible, then it will be vital to provide a map with clear instructions and directions. Guests who are new to the area may know you and your home well, but not the village hall or a hotel miles from anywhere.

The important decisions taken, it is then time to think about the style of the wedding and the finance. The date that has been set will determine the season, such as spring or autumn, and this can influence the style of dress designs, colourings and flowers. The next consideration is the size of wedding, and the number of attendants. Who is to make the cake? The dresses? The posies? The lists are seemingly endless, but they are essential, and before all is over there will be lists of lists, and lists of lists of lists!

Collecting Ideas

There are some very good wedding guides that are inexpensive and well worth buying; they will certainly ensure that nothing is forgotten! It is always a good idea to record ideas from magazines, books or other weddings that you may have seen, to help in the decisions that have to be made about the dress, the style for the attendants and the decorations. It is not wrong to use other people's ideas; it is more than likely that they took them from somewhere else also! Collecting ideas will help you to formulate your preferred designs, which will then make it easy to work on from that point, rather than having nothing to get the adrenalin flowing. Don't be persuaded by others; listen to their advice but let the decisions be your own.

From here it is with flowers and foliages that I will suggest ideas and schemes, but remember that a wedding is seen as a whole, and in limited time and space coordination is very important to create a lovely feeling of totality of design.

The blueprint established and colleagues approached, it is time to relax a little, until the meetings with the dressmaker, the caterer, the printer, the car-hire firm, the photographer and the flower people . . . And then we can begin.

A winter design with foliages and beautiful colourings to enhance the Nativity scene in the stained-glass window. Candles have been included in the design, but they can easily be removed, if necessary, as they have been placed in candleholders, pushed into the floral foam.

An Overall Plan

If you are the mother or guardian of the bride and are responsible for everything concerning the wedding, then much planning and detailed organization will be required. If you do not prepare, it will be a very harassed and unhappy time for all concerned.

Being responsible for everything is possible, but doing it alone is not. There are many friends and relations who will happily give their services if invited to do so, and it is good to work as a team, but careful planning is needed. List the requirements, try to estimate the time needed to accomplish each one, and work from there.

Making the wedding cake and decorating it will take time, but this can be done well ahead of the day. Dresses to be made can again be worked beforehand, but help here is also useful (and sewing parties can be great fun). Even a non-sewing friend will happily make the coffee. However, there is one item on the agenda that has to be dealt with the day before the wedding, when there are so many other things to cope with – the flowers. Do not attempt to work on these all alone! There is usually a flower guild in the church who can help and many friends will be more than willing to lend a hand.

Unless it is absolutely vital to arrange the floristry yourself, then this is the time to use a professional florist or a friend who is able. Remember that headdresses and posies are time-consuming. Although some simple ideas are shown in the book, these designs can only be worked on the day of, or the night before, the wedding, when all is usually at its most hectic.

The flowers for the church and the reception can be arranged a day or so before the wedding if needed, but very careful conditioning is necessary and again it makes good sense to enlist help.

The Flowers and Foliages

The flowers and the foliages will have to be picked or purchased, preferably three days before the wedding and possibly longer if special lilies are to be used. These will have to be conditioned and placed in buckets in a cool place to await arrangement. Floral foam is easier to manage if soaked ahead of time, allowed to dry a little and then put into a plastic bag to keep moist; the foam will then simply require refreshing before being placed in the receptacles for the arrangements. The damp foam will be quite heavy to carry, so a helpful husband or two can be roped in here to help.

Do not be tempted to arrange the most important designs yourself, as in the excitement they could well not come up to your expectations. Instead, choose something special, such as the design on the table in the vestry or where the Register will be signed, or perhaps a basket arrangement in the porch which can be a gift for a granny or the 'other mother' after the service. If flower-arranging friends or the church flower guild have been chosen to help, then allocating each an arrangement will be simplicity itself. The provision of wet floral foam, wire netting, tape and flowers – and, of course, a cup of tea or coffee and perhaps a biscuit or two, to help to keep the spirits high – is all that will be required. It is a good idea to appear half-way through the arranging time with the refreshments, to encourage everyone to take a 'breather' and a cup of coffee, and to look at the progress being made. This way you can ensure that all is going 'according to plan' and the team are happy.

There are always very special friends who will ask if they can help in any way. Give them the opportunity to show their kindness and enlist their help in clearing and tidying up afterwards. Arranging flowers is often quite tiring and a spare pair of hands or so at the end is more than welcome. It is also a good idea to ask for help with the watering, 'topping up' and spraying that will be necessary before leaving and if possible on the morning of the wedding day.

Possible Problems

The reception can present a problem if it is not possible to decorate the venue before the actual day. However, you could always arrange the table posies at home, again with help if you can find it, leaving just a special design for the receiving line and the top table or buffet table. With or without help, these can be worked while the tables are being put up and laid by helpers. It is surprising how useful the family can be at this time!

If the reception is at home, then things will be a little easier. Do try to allow some time to have a short break, though, even if it is only in the bath – and do stipulate that at such times the bathroom is just for you only. It is good to have quiet time to be alone before such a special day.

Delegation

From a purely practical point of view I would suggest that the flowers for a wedding are best left to a professional florist, a friend who is a flower arranger or the church flower guild. If any or all of these options are chosen, you will still be left with the most important part – the planning and choice of colour schemes that are to be used. It is, of course, possible to help with the arrangements, but leaving the main bulk of the flowers to be arranged by others is much the better scheme.

An important point to establish early in the planning time is the system of flower arranging used in the church of your choice; the reception venue will invariably be that of your own choosing. When the date for the wedding is being discussed with the priest, as well as any other special requirements, such as the bells or the choir, it is sensible to check about the flowers: will you be allowed a free hand to place the designs where you please or are there restrictions? It is often the wish of the priest that flowers are not placed on the altar. If this is so, then you must abide by his decision, however much you would like to see two elegant designs placed there.

It might also be the case that only the flower guild are allowed to arrange in the church, although this is very rarely the situation. (Most flower guilds are quite happy to have a weekend off!) If only the guild are permitted to arrange the flowers, it is quite in order for you to request special colourings and flowers. This does not guarantee that you will have exactly what you want, but it will help the guild in their choice of materials. Payment will of course be expected.

If it is your choice to arrange the flowers and you are able to do so, then there are several important details to bear in mind: the availability of containers, water and access to the church, for example. You will need to know where a key can be obtained and who to contact in an emergency. Will the flowers be required afterwards or must they be cleared quickly? (This can sometimes be the case with a wedding in Lent, if the vicar has kindly allowed flowers for the ceremony.) What time will you be able to get into the church to start the arrangements and are there any special services during the day that might involve your having to stop for a while? It is also sensible to allow for services which cannot be anticipated. I well remember a flower festival that had to be interrupted while a funeral service was taken. No amount of planning can prevent such things, but a little thought ahead of time will spare great agonizings if and when they do occur.

Collate Ideas

The options will now be clear and the choice is yours. Next the plans need to be set in order. If a professional florist is to be used, then a meeting will have to be arranged and all the relevant information given. Colour snippets of the materials and styles will have to be discussed and any special flowers that are desired will need to be noted. The only limitation that perhaps might follow is one of finance.

If the flower guild have agreed to arrange the flowers, a letter from you will be needed to advise both them and the vicar. If possible, it is a good idea to meet and discuss the arrangements and ideas you have in mind. If this is not feasible, then again some snippets of the materials and the colours and flowers required are useful. It is not very sensible to expect roses, lilies or orchids if your donation is to be a small one. It is important to be realistic.

Combining Forces

One very happy option is to work with the flower guild and say that you will supply all the flowers needed while perhaps they might help with foliages from the garden. This is often a most satisfactory approach from all points of view. The flower guild will be familiar with their church and the whereabouts of special containers, the water supply and the rubbish tip - all very useful information that will help to keep everyone happy and things running smoothly.

OPPOSITE *The pew end design here is delightfully light and delicate. The materials include berries, grasses and interesting pieces of foliage that are just caught with changing autumn tints. Old man's beard which has been glycerined is a lovely addition to the design.*

Unless it is your own place of worship do remember that the church in which the flowers are to be arranged has a team of people who work very hard each week to keep it looking beautiful. It is not very thoughtful to barge in and take over! Criticism of containers or the arrangements found there is very unkind and, as a guest in the church, very discourteous.

Another happy idea for help with flowers is to call in local flower or garden clubs. There are many such organizations that would be willing to help, and some I know work only for a donation to charity - a very worthwhile way of helping those in need.

Liaising Help to Avoid the Pitfalls

Whatever decision you take as to the arrangers, it is good to follow my suggestions for liaising with the flower guild so as to ensure a happy time for everyone, with no 'hiccups' on the day. I know of one instance when the bride, who had not asked if pew ends were allowed, found to her dismay that those lovingly made arrangements had been removed. If she had taken the trouble to check, the reply would have been a firm but kindly refusal, for a simple reason: the pew ends had been badly water-stained by previous decorations and it had taken much time and effort to restore them. In all cases, it is not only good manners but also sound common sense to get the 'go-ahead' before plunging in at the deep end with enthusiastic fervour.

Reception Flowers

The flowers for the reception will also need to be discussed and will depend greatly on the venue and the time allotted for the arranging. The manager of a hotel will happily take on the responsibility for you, yours to command. Here your only part is to write the cheque, having given him the details. It will also be possible to have some of the flowers worked by the hotel and some by you, with help of course. (It is nigh on impossible to arrange flowers at the reception, rush off to change and then go on to the church . . . It has been done, but only with much pre-planning and great difficulty.) A flower-arranging friend and your friends will almost certainly help, and it will just fall to you to bring coffee, grateful thanks and praise.

It is a very good idea to write to the hotel manager with all the details that have been decided, including any collections that will be required after the wedding of your containers, pinholders and suchlike. The pedestals will be relatively easy to track down but the precious pinholders and weights will have been thrown away with the flowers and the dustbins long emptied! (Do I sound as though I am speaking from bitter experience? Rest assured that I certainly am!)

The organization of the arrangements is now well in hand and discussions on the colour, style and finance will follow. I do have just one last request for the bride and her mother: if possible, pop in during the time of arranging to say a friendly 'hello`. I know that you will have a thousand and one other things to do, but the pleasure it gives to those working on your behalf is immeasurable. (Besides, I am sure you will want to see what the arrangements look like as well!) Of course, they will be just as lovely as you envisaged – probably even better – and how lovely for a mother to sit quietly with her daughter in the church where, on the following day, the girl will be a radiant and happy bride. It could well be that eyes will become very misty and the flowers no more than a haze of colour on the day . . . What a pity to have missed them!

CHECKLIST

DECIDE ON THE DATE, TIME AND VENUE OF THE
CEREMONY AND THE RECEPTION

MAKE AN OVERALL PLAN FOR THE WEDDING

KEEP A NOTE OF PREFERRED STYLES, COLOURS AND DESIGNS

DRAW UP A TIMETABLE AND SEND A SCHEDULE TO
EVERYONE INVOLVED

MAKE CONTACT WITH THE CHURCH FLOWER GUILD
OR LOCAL FLOWER CLUB

WRITE TO THE MANAGER OF THE RECEPTION VENUE
TO CONFIRM ARRANGEMENTS

2

SETTING THE FLORAL SCENE

ONCE YOU HAVE YOUR 'SETTING' in mind, it is a good idea to sit there quietly, just to get the feel of the building, its size and atmosphere. All places of worship have something special and unique unto themselves and it is lovely when the decorations are in harmony. The small, intimate building will not look at its best if it has been crammed to over-flowing with grand and opulent designs; equally, the smart town venue will look a little uncomfortable if decorated as for a country wedding. Your aim is to suit the style to the situation, using coordination and good taste. The colouring of the architecture will change with the seasons and it is wise to try to remember this when making a visit. If the day is very bright and sunny when reconnoitring but the wedding is to be in the winter, do not think about the flowers that will be right for the present time but look ahead to dark, dreary days and plan accordingly; lemon and pale blue may well be perfect for the spring or summer, but on a cold day, with grey stone walls, that particular colour scheme could be very bleak.

Enhancing, Not Hiding

Remember that the main reason for flower decoration is to enhance and not to hide everything and everyone behind vast displays; it is there especially to add to the joy of the day. This can be achieved in many ways, but to get the right balance requires a little thought and some planning.

Anyone can place a few flowers in a stand and the effect will no doubt be attractive, but with a little thought as to coordination with the colours to be worn by the bridal party and the creation of designs that suit the style of the church you will be able to create something truly splendid. Weddings are always very special occasions and are very happily remembered, but with that extra effort they can be unforgettable!

The first consideration must be the size of the wedding. Is it to be a very large occasion, with all the family and friends, or a small, intimate affair, with only those closely concerned with the bride and groom? Many factors will contribute to the style, and the exciting thing is that each wedding will be unique. Religion, lifestyle, finance and particular dreams will all play a very large part in forming the final decisions.

Unless there is very little time available before the wedding day, it is well worth pondering at length on the most suitable style with a sensible budget in mind. It is necessary to decide on the amount of money to be spent and then allocate it, rather than making very elaborate designs which will overstretch the finances. Setting your sights at the right level will avoid much heartache. The main point to remember is that the marriage service is the most important part of all; after that, everything else will fall into place.

Advice

There are so many styles and types of wedding that it is impossible to generalize. The best sources for advice will be found in the many books and magazines that have been published on the subject. These can be readily purchased or borrowed from a library. Consulting two or three sources is preferable as it allows comparisons to be made and will give you a range of ideas.

Discuss your ideas with others who have had previous wedding experience, and even visit places where you know that there will be ceremonies. This will help you to get an idea of the needs and scope of the situation. Of course, every wedding will be different and have its own special features, but this will help to get things into perspective.

Weather

Unpredictable weather is always a problem and it is wise to prepare for such an eventuality. Small, pretty tents and awnings can be hired and very effectively decorated to continue the garden theme. Unless the garden is very sheltered, the tent or awning will act as a good wind-break and provide welcome shade if it is very hot.

Timing

It is always a good idea to get the outline plans well under way and then have time to sit back and rethink if necessary. I usually find that my

first thoughts are my best but that they are improved and strengthened with thoughts at a later stage, when the initial ideas have had time to be absorbed and mulled over. Lists and a notebook are invaluable.

Atmosphere

The flower arrangements will add greatly to the atmosphere and ambience of the day, and the choice of colour and flowers will certainly help to create a distinctive style. Colour is often determined purely by the bridal scheme and is a delight if well coordinated. However, it is important to choose carefully to avoid blandness: do not use exactly the same colour for all the flowers. It is lovely to find one or two types of flower that match the bridesmaid dresses, but it is always worthwhile to search for others that will complement or tone with the scheme, to bring greater interest and a better finished result.

The use of colour can greatly influence the occasion. Yellows and lemons are uplifting; whites, creams and pastel shades have luminosity and are very useful if the venues are dark or cramped. The choice of foliages will also be

OPPOSITE *Always a very attractive feature, the lych gate here has been decorated with garlands and swags with lovely autumnal colourings. The garlands have been tied up with string and securely fastened in the event of inclement weather. Nails and wire are not needed, nor are they good for the old wooden structure.*

OVERLEAF *The beautiful screen that divides the nave from the chancel has been decorated with arrangements worked in floral packs hooked on to the wooden tracery. (The hooks have been bound with tape to prevent any damage to the screen. The floral foam pack was well soaked and then allowed to dry a little to prevent any water-staining to the wood.) Winter foliages and berries of all kinds, with winter white flowers, have been loosely arranged in the foam packs, with ivies gently following the curves of the screen. An alternative idea could be to garland the screen with foliages and berries.*

Such winter wedding designs are the perfect foil to the elegant screen and guide the eye through to the altar beyond.

important and can make or mar the designs. For me, the foliage is as important as the flowers themselves, and certainly one of my main concerns.

Suitable to the Setting

When setting the scene – and this is very much the same for a film or stage director – the idea is to create appropriate arrangements for the venue and the occasion. The arrangements should look comfortable in the setting and not overpower or detract from the bridal party or the place of the marriage. Consideration for the overall appearance is paramount.

Attention to detail when setting the scene brings a personal touch and is always noticed. It creates a good feeling. Pew ends with some unusual foliages or flowers will be seen at close quarters and subtly convey the care that has gone into the designs, making everything so special for the occasion.

The Personal Approach

A wedding is obviously a very important day and probably the one on which the most care and attention, not to say money, will be

OPPOSITE *A mossed garland has been used with twigs and spring flowers. Primulas, still in their plastic pots, have been wired into the design. (If the pots are of the heavy terracotta type the plants can be placed into small plastic bags and then wired into the garland.) The flowers and foliage have been set into the damp moss.*

In the background can be seen the font and windowsill, also decorated with spring flowers. The design for the font has been worked in a 'continental style', using all white flowers. The windowsill has the interesting addition of small terracotta pots, some of which hold similar plants to those used in the garland.

expended. It is important to have everything just right – which means right for the individual. A petite bride will need flowers that show her to advantage; large, heavy designs will overwhelm, whereas dainty, exquisite flowers will accentuate her fragile appearance. The same design, however beautiful, will be lost on a bride of more comfortable proportions, but an elegant sheaf of lilies or a spray which falls enchantingly will look stunning. A good way to assess the suitability of a design is to make a mock arrangement in silk or dried flowers, or perhaps just to use fresh foliage of the style and size preferred, and to hold it in front of a mirror to get the general feeling. It will quickly be apparent if the size and style are correct. Some florists have books of designs to look at, but these cannot really show how a particular arrangement will suit an individual. Sometimes the florist will have silk designs to help you reach a decision.

Lighting

I do not advocate lighting the wedding as for a stage set, but if the venues are very dark it might be worth investigating the possibility of additional lighting. The placing of a light behind a pedestal design can certainly look very effective and will lighten the area considerably. Placing lights under trees or archways will also bring the extra light needed and add greatly to the designs. As setting the scene is so important, attention to such matters as lighting, which will not be costly, will certainly add to the effect.

Using the Decorations to Advantage

No situation is perfect and there are often unsightly parts that need to be hidden. Clever

The wedding cake has been decorated with small versions of the bouquet, which have been set into the cake in small plastic tubes.

positioning of flower designs will solve the problem easily. Do not spend time and precious finance trying to cover the offending eyesore; simply place the designs a little way away from the problem and no one will notice it.

Conversely, there are often some very attractive parts of a building that are well worth drawing attention to, such as a beautiful window or archway. Here, carefully thought-out designs to enhance them will be a delight. Do not be tempted to over-decorate such an area or the object of the exercise will be lost.

A Wedding Theme

Wedding dreams take many forms and fulfilling them can be a joy. In earlier years, the Victorian bride would simply have worn a dress of the period, carrying a simple posy and wearing a bonnet that had perhaps been decorated. Today a bride will often wish to choose a wedding theme from any one of a number of historical periods and plan her clothes and decorations accordingly. Take, for example, the 'Gainsborough' theme: you could use soft garden designs in baskets, with delicate colourings and beautiful full-blown roses and peonies in abundance. Or a 'twenties' theme, with simple stylish designs. The list is virtually endless, and great fun to do.

If a period theme is planned, then attention to detail is very important. A Victorian bridesmaid will look lovely with a decorated muff or bonnet, but not with a modern flower ball.

The library is an excellent source for ideas on period details and there have been several books written on period flowers that will help with the correct choice. The colour will be especially important to note and will ensure that the whole scheme is well coordinated. A period theme is charming, but it does have to be right to create a good end result.

A period wedding is not suitable for everyone – and how marvellous that there is scope for such differing ideas – but whether choosing a period theme or not, a colour scheme is very pleasing. A wedding that has been designed with colour in mind brings a lovely feeling of togetherness, which is obviously the perfect atmosphere to create at a wedding.

The Seasons

The seasons will influence the choice of flowers and sometimes the choice of colouring, although in these days of fast air travel there are very few flowers not available all the year round. The only problem of choosing flowers 'out of season' is one of cost. The colour of the bride's hair can also be a deciding factor; redheads in particular are especially fortunate here. If pink is a favourite colour of the bride, then 'go for it', but look at the varying shades that can be used to give interest and variety. Choose foliages that are unusual or those that will give a distinct outline to the design.

For this one day, and perhaps never again, the bride will be the centre of attention; it is a day when every detail will be under close scrutiny. The average will doubtless be lovely, but some especially unusual flower or enchanting design will be much admired and remembered always as a highlight. Every leaf will be recorded by the photographer. This is a challenge for everyone concerned, but particularly for the flower arranger. Faults are always so noticeable and can spoil the most beautiful of work.

No one thing is or ever can be perfect, but attention to conditioning, style and good taste, with a desire for distinction, will bring the very best results, which are always so very well worthwhile.

CHECKLIST

PLANNING THE DESIGNS SUITABLE TO THE SETTING

CREATING THE BEST EFFECT FOR THE SITUATION

WEDDING THEMES AND APPROPRIATE FLOWERS

ATTENTION TO DETAIL

3

COORDINATION

WITH THE STYLE, perhaps a period theme and certainly the date and venues decided, it is time for all those involved in the wedding plans to meet with the bride and her mother. It is a good idea to set aside some time to discuss the details, but not with everyone together, however convenient this might seem to the bride and her mother. Each part of the wedding plan will need to be worked individually, unless there are some overlaps – for example, the hat made by the milliner that is to be decorated by the florist. Time allocated for each one now will certainly save confusion later.

Wherever the meeting takes place, try not to hurry through it, fidgeting to get away to the next appointment. Good results are never achieved when trying to think about or work on several things at the same time. It is a very good move to have both the mother of the bride and the bride at the meeting, as the young have very positive ideas on what they do and do not like, and often the bride does not have an opportunity to express an opinion until it is too late, mother having made all the plans without her. It is the bride's day and her wishes should be considered. If the meeting is not to be at the home of the bride, she should bring any relevant items, such as magazine cuttings or photographs of other weddings with designs that are preferred and snippets of the materials that will be used for the dresses.

Listen carefully to the bride and her mother and jot down any details that are important. Make a note of any queries that crop up as a result of their comments. From this information much will have been gathered as to the colour, style and type of wedding that is planned.

The optimum time to have such a meeting is about four or five months before the wedding day.

Questions Needing Answers

A number of questions will invariably arise from listening to the bride, but there will also be several vital details required from the flower-arranging point of view. The discussions will have revealed the proposed size and scale of the wedding, and it is important that if the suggested flower designs are too many or too complicated, this is stated immediately. Then there will be plenty of time to either rethink the designs or find another florist. It is never easy to admit defeat before the race, but it is most important that this is made clear, rather than battling on with disastrous results.

If the designs and ideas are well able to be worked, then the next question must be that of the finance allocated for the flowers. If the proposed funding seems insufficient, this must be discussed immediately, and either a less ambitious scheme chosen or the finances reviewed.

It is often a surprise to people who are not involved with flower arranging or floristry that the lovely decorations, so tantalizingly shown in magazines, although very simple in appearance are often complicated to work, needing an army of skilled arrangers to create them, and that the seemingly casual posy of garden flowers is one of the most laborious designs to make, and even more difficult to keep fresh. It is sometimes the case that flowers for a wedding are considered the one area in which economies can be made and yet even so a magnificent display is still expected. There are ways to economize, but skimped flowers are dreadful and it is better to have one stunning design than attempt to create several arrangements with an inadequate budget. Sensible discussion will resolve the problem.

Fulfilling Special Needs

There is one other request that is often made, and that is 'for something different'. I must admit to enjoying new and exciting 'way-out' designs, but I do feel that a wedding is not really the right time for the extraordinary. Weddings can, of course, have decorations just as the bride wishes (assuming that the vicar is in agreement), but this is a very beautiful, thoughtful and romantic time, so stiff or contorted 'space-age' designs are perhaps inappropriate. However, I think that maybe the request is a call for help and in the main the plea is to avoid the inevitable pedestal with a stiff triangle of florist flowers perched primly on the top. Decidedly dull, and certainly not fulfilling the desire for 'thoughtfully beautiful designs'.

There are many lovely alternative ideas for the pedestal arrangement, and most are probably less expensive to make than a 'triangle' of florist flowers. An arrangement of all foliages in variety, flowing naturally and elegantly, can be a very easy alternative. Remember, though, that if a professional florist is asked for such a design, it could well be as costly as one with flowers; living in a town or city can also create a problem for such designs. There are, however, many florists who do sell good foliages, and they are certainly obtainable from the market.

Colour Accents

A wedding that has been haphazardly put together will certainly give just such an appearance, however beautiful the bride and the flowers. A colour scheme is always a good way to link the whole and bring harmony to the scene. The colour chosen for the time of year is important, although the perennial favourite colours of pink and white still prevail. (Peach has enjoyed considerable popularity since a certain Royal wedding.) The choice of colour must be, of course, the special preference of the bride, and certainly this can vary from red to purple, through to black!

The time of year is really, I feel, the best angle from which to work. Spring weddings are perhaps the easiest to plan, with all the wonderful fresh colourings after the winter. I am always surprised how often the glorious yellows and lemons of spring are ignored by spring brides, in favour of pink or peach. From a purely practical point of view, the flowers found so freely at this time of the year are much cheaper and, for me, more appropriate. Primroses in baskets for pew ends are a joy . . . and there is certainly no other time in the year when these can be used. The summer rosy pinks are just as wonderful and the glow of full-blown garden roses and their perfume are indeed perfection.

Of course, each season has very special plant materials that are particular to that time and I love to see seasonal flowers used in their own times. From a practical point of view, the financial benefit from less expensive materials is much to be recommended; and somehow the right flowers in the right season bring a feeling of 'correctness', the light and the ambience enhancing the atmosphere and excitement. Autumnal colourings will always look sensational in the autumn, but will look a little too exotic for winter or spring decorations.

Take time to look at other wedding colour

A BASKET SHOWER

The basket is set upon a wooden pillar. Floral foam and wire netting are used as the mechanics and a plastic bowl is placed inside first if there is not a plastic liner.

The design is created by commencing with long trailing pieces flowing down at the front, and slowly building up the flowers and foliages. The back of the design is not high, and to ensure that the visual balance is correct some heavier materials should be used there. From a very practical point of view, a heavy weight is a good idea placed at the back of the basket, just in case!

schemes in books or magazines, and note how the weather, the light and suchlike will affect the colourings that have been used.

The church colourings can have an influence on the scheme. If there is a very strong element, such as a deep-blue carpet or bright-red hassocks, these might well need to be considered. Collecting together the relevant details will help to determine the colour scheme. If all this seems a little pedantic, the end result will amply justify the time taken to 'get it right'. There is only one day . . . and it has to be flawless.

The Flower Choice

The colour scheme decided, the flowers are the next 'hurdle' to tackle. Again the seasons can influence the choice, although with modern transport and in this day and age of 'fast everything', almost every kind of flower is obtainable throughout the year. As a sensible suggestion and from a financial angle, seasonal flowers are usually less expensive and more readily available. It is always very disappointing to have to say, though it is quite reasonable, that one must be flexible when choosing flowers; the weather, availability in the market, late or early seasons and perhaps cost can all be factors which will affect the choice. This is a good reason to leave the flower selection until about six weeks to a month before the day, as the state of the season will be apparent by this time.

The number of arrangements and the time allowed in which to arrange them are important. If, for example, the flowers have to be arranged three days before the wedding (sometimes unavoidable with special services), then sturdy, long-lasting flowers are essential and very good conditioning of any slightly suspect subjects absolutely vital.

The all-year-round chrysanthemums are

extremely reliable flowers, although perhaps a little dull, and certainly carnations are always a safe bet. Hopefully, though, this will not be a problem that has to be faced, and the arrangements can be worked according to schedule.

The shower design has been used to decorate the small chapel. Two large blocks of floral foam, one upright and one flat and covered with wire netting, have been placed in a plastic container. The style and the containers are very appropriate here and create a feeling of delightful simplicity.

A PEDESTAL DESIGN SHOWN IN STAGES

1. *Floral foam set on to foam holder.*
2. *Wire netting placed over and wired securely.*
3. *The outline of the design is created with foliages. The focal point of the arrangement must be used to help with the design, and the lines of the materials should all radiate from this imaginary position. Stems should not cross each other, causing a muddled appearance. A hard outline should be avoided, if possible, unless of course a stiff pyramid is desired. Pedestal designs are an elegant form of decoration and a gentle flowing design is usually a good choice.*

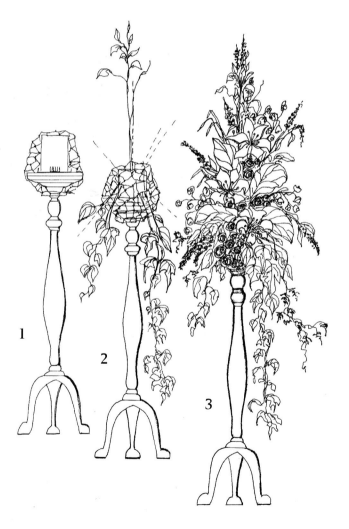

Assessing the Flower Order

The number of flowers will have to be assessed, allowing for a few over – accidents do happen and it is important to order at least four or five extra of each type of flower to avoid any problems (two extra lilies will suffice). Plan sensibly and do not over-order excessively; too many flowers look as bad as too few. A typical pedestal arrangement for an altar design will require approximately the following:

> 3 long sprays of trailing material (e.g. ivy)
> 5 or 7 large sprays of foliage
> 5 large leaves (e.g. hosta or similar)
> 10 pieces of smaller foliage or blossom
> 7 long-stemmed flowers (e.g. *Alstroemeria*)
> 5 intermediate-sized flowers (e.g. carnations)
> 3 large important flowers (e.g. lilies)

This number and these types of material are quite sufficient to give a really good arrangement, without cramming the container to overflowing. 'Allowing room for the butterflies' is a flower arranger's quotation, well worth remembering.

With this simple example and the designs illustrated, it should be quite easy to calculate the amount required. Then, 'shop around' for cost and available sources of the materials required. Get an estimate, or two if the order is to be a large one. When satisfied, a firm order should be placed, with a contingency plan for acceptable alternatives. Not many florists require payment in advance; this is not always possible anyway, but some may ask for a deposit. (This is really only fair for the small florist, who will normally hold just a small amount of stock.) It should be paid promptly

OPPOSITE *The tall, elegant pedestal arrangements will frame the bride and groom during the marriage ceremony. The designs have been created as a background, not overpowering but enhancing the setting.*

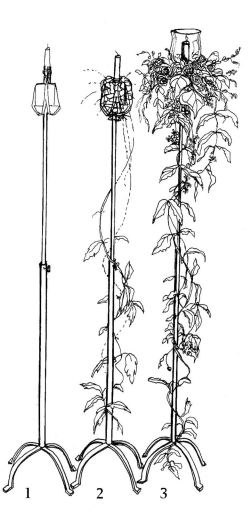

TALL PEW END DESIGNS

Tall adjustable stands were made as an alternative design for pew ends and with the idea of using them as candleholders.
1. Floral foam is placed in the dish and taped securely.
2. Wire netting is laid over the foam and wired firmly in place. Long trailing pieces of foliage are allowed to curl attractively around and down the tall support.
3. The design is completed with flowers and foliages. A candle is set in a holder and pushed into the floral foam, and a hurricane glass is placed over the candle and pressed well down also. For additional security the candle and glass can be taped.

by the father of the bride, or whoever is responsible for the bills, and a gentle reminder at this stage that a cheque will be required before the wedding for the flowers is always a good idea.

Containers for the Arrangements

The containers to be used for the flowers need to be considered. If those already in the church are available for use, then a visit to the flower cupboard with the flower guild lady is a good idea. Check on the mechanics needed for each vase to be used and jot down in that now quite well-worn notebook the needs for each one. Do not leave this to your memory or hope that your helpers will be fully competent flower arrangers; the mechanics are the most important part of the exercise.

The amounts of floral foam, netting, tape and wire that are needed can be assessed at this stage and purchased in readiness. Allow at least three extra blocks of floral foam and spare wire netting for the sudden extra arrangement or accident that might happen. (In the excitement I have known floral foam to collapse under the hands of the over-enthusiastic arranger or the inexperienced one who continually changes her mind about the position of a special flower or pushes a large branch into the middle of the design.)

Essential Mechanics

Purchasing a box of floral foam is generally cheaper, and likewise buying a roll of wire netting. I prefer the green plastic-covered type,

OPPOSITE *The aisle has been transformed with these tall designs, leading the eye to the similar designs on either side of the altar.*

PEDESTAL DESIGNS

Pedestals are useful for arrangements that are very important or need to be free-standing. The following are some of the many styles that can be used.

1. *Pillars – plastic, marble, wood, stone or terracotta.*
2. *Wrought iron – many styles, mostly adjustable.*
3. *Torchère or adapted lamp standard – wood.*
4. *Low table or bird bath – stone, plastic, wood.*
5. *Figure supporting a dish – plastic, wood, stone, marble.*
6. *Ash-tray stand – wood, metal.*
7. *Suitable mechanics for all the designs.*

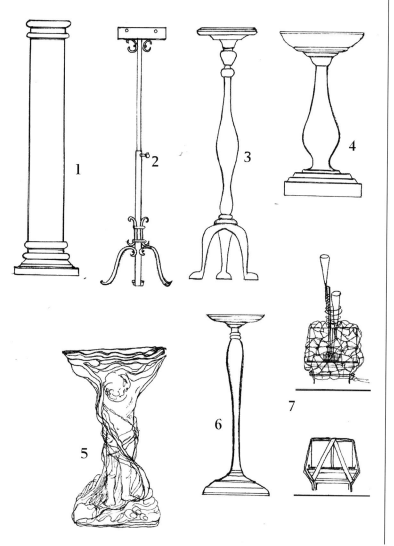

with at least 1½ inch mesh, from an ironmonger, rather than the individual pieces from a florist. This will only really be necessary if the wedding is a very large one. However, if flower arranging is part of your lifestyle, then both will be more than useful in the months to come. Oasis tape is a boon, especially the thin dark-green variety; canes and cones are also useful if the designs are to be very large. Preparing these in advance is always a good idea when time is at a premium.

Soaking the floral foam ahead of the arranging day is always sensible. It will be necessary to check on the type of foam that is being used, as some need much less time to absorb water than others. Soak the foam and then allow it to drain a little before placing it in plastic bags until required. Preparing the foam in this way will save much mess and time on the day; certainly, soaking foam in a small sink in the vestry or in the kitchen or cloakroom of the reception venue is never a very good idea. The containers with the wet foam will be quite heavy and need to be in stout plastic bags. A note on the handle of the bags containing the foam is a good idea to prevent it being squashed. Enthusiastic helpers are not always aware of the possible pitfalls with wet foam!

Useful Props

A very useful prop for arranging is a basket or box in which to keep scissors, wires, string and so on. It is particularly handy also to include the First Aid Kit here, and a flask for hot water. No, not the coffee in this one; it is for the revival of any 'fallen flowers'. (See pages 34–5, Conditioning the Flowers and Foliage.)

If the bridal flowers are to be worked, then all the necessary wires and accessories must be purchased. Maybe hoops or baskets are required. Take time to find the best size and perhaps one that is extra-prettily shaped. Any ribbons wanted should be acquired at this stage and not a day or so before they are needed. Planning ahead will give you the time to acquire 'just the right colour', rather than having to find one that will 'do' at the last minute.

This is the time also to liaise with the milliner and/or the dressmaker. The dress fabrics will already have been noted, but if the bride is wearing a hat which is to be decorated with flowers, then close cooperation will be needed. Perhaps the bridesmaids are to carry decorated muffs. Then the dressmaker will have to be consulted as to the best way of attaching the flower designs. Leaving such things until the last minute is courting disaster.

The Flower Arrangers

If there is to be one, a flower-arranging team will need to be briefed for the wedding arrangements, and it will certainly make life very much easier for all concerned if a plan of action is worked through carefully ahead of time. It is not necessary to have everyone to a site meeting, unless the occasion is a very large one with many designs to be worked. A chat over a cup of tea or coffee will be very helpful

and will also establish the amount of help available and the ability of the arrangers. The volunteers might well only be capable of very simple table designs and allocating designs beyond their capabilities will cause much worry, for all concerned.

A timetable and a schedule for each member of your team might seem to be a little fussy, but it really is worthwhile and prevents any mishaps, such as turning up a day late! It is also very useful to send a simple map, showing car-parking. There will inevitably be much to transport and it is always a help to have extra hands to fetch and carry, and car owners who will transport flowers etc. A list of what needs to be taken is useful and then each item can be crossed off as it is loaded into a car. This is a wise precaution, for in the bustle it is easy to leave something behind and this could well be a disaster, especially if the location is a considerable distance away.

Help with conditioning the plant materials is a boon, but ensure that those who offer have the know-how!

So, with everything planned, the ideas well coordinated and the team prepared and eager for action, all now should be in complete readiness for Arranging Day.

CHECKLIST

DISCUSSIONS WITH ALL THE PARTIES CONCERNED

COSTING AND FINANCIAL PLANNING

COLOUR

FLOWER CHOICE

MECHANICS

4

THE WEDDING WEEK

THE DESIGNS AND FLOWERS planned, the coordination of the final details for arranging them must now be the prime task. Flower buckets, as many as possible (friends will most certainly help out here), need to be gathered in the place where the flowers are to be conditioned and held in readiness for arranging. A garage, if it can be spared, is a very good location, and does save a lot of mess and water in the house. If the flowers and foliages have to be in the kitchen, then a large plastic sheet on the floor will be very useful and save a lot of clearing-up time at a later stage. The best buckets to use are those with solid side handles which allow them to be carried with two hands, with the flowers or foliages safe from decapitation. However, any bucket is better than no bucket and at a time when many flowers and much foliage will need to be kept in water, every kind will be a great help. I often use the bath for soaking, but this can cause problems.

The amount of floral foam to be used, previously estimated, has to be soaked. An old tin or baby bath is ideal, and allows a considerable number of blocks to be soaked at the same time. Once soaked – and it is important to check on the length of time needed for this exercise, as some types take much longer than others (the instructions are usually on the side of the box) – the foam can be placed in plastic bags to retain moisture. It is a good idea to drain the foam a little, as it is very heavy when fully charged with water. As long as the foam remains damp, it is very simple to recharge it when needed for the arrangements.

Pre-plans and Preparations

If it is possible to put the foam and wire netting in the containers, this will certainly save time on the arranging day. However, this must be sanctioned by the church and the reception venue. I often like to work some of the foliages at this time, and find it a great boon when there is much to do. Some people describe this as 'greening up'.

Conditioning the Flowers and Foliages

If flowers and foliages are from the garden, then they must be picked either early or late in the day. Do not attempt to pick in the height of summer in the middle of a hot day or the flowers and foliages will have wilted before you can put them into water. It is a good idea to take a bucket with you containing some water, into which you can place the freshly picked materials. This method certainly is very useful for young and tender specimens. Then, having picked all that is required, they must be conditioned. This applies equally to the florist flowers that you have collected or had delivered. Conditioning is important to ensure that the flowers and foliages are at their best and stay that way. Skipping this process will inevitably cause problems. For the uninitiated, conditioning is a way (and there are many different methods than can be used) of preparing the plant materials so that they take up water readily in order to stay fresh and looking good. The simplest method is to cut the ends of the stems at an angle and give them a long, cool drink in deep water before arranging. Two hours is the very minimum time and overnight is preferable. For certain materials I have included the types of conditioning best suited to their needs; the Index of Flowers and Foliages can be found at the back of the book (see pages 94–5).

Keep a Checklist

Check that all necessary items, such as tape, wires, string and so on, are in a box or basket, plus the sticking plasters and, of course, *flower scissors*, two pairs if possible, as one usually has a happy knack of losing itself in the foliage! You will also need large plastic sheets and dust sheets, brushes and dustpans, mops and dusters, with a flask of hot water for 'flower repairs'. Any ladders or steps that will be needed can quite easily be transported on the roof rack of a car, but it is sound sense to inquire if there are any available for you to use in the church. It does seem as though you will be taking everything but the kitchen sink . . . but it will all be needed.

Something for the Inner Man!

A flask of coffee or tea and a packet of biscuits are always on my list, and I know many will include a sandwich or two so as to keep hunger at bay!

Packing the Car

It is wise to pack all the non-perishable items in the car the night before arranging day, leaving ample space for the flowers. The flowers will travel happily in flower boxes, perhaps those in which they came, or in buckets. There

ALTAR DESIGN

1. *The base and the plastic urn have been painted to give a stone-type finish. A wooden construction has been made to fit inside the urn, into which the dishes to hold the floral foam are placed. The foam has been taped in position with floral tape.*
2. *Wire netting secured with wire is placed over the foam. This will be needed to help support the heavy materials that will be used. Florist cones taped to garden canes are pushed into the top layer and well secured with tape.*
3. *The small outline drawings suggest suitable shapes for a finished design; the one with the cross advises guarding against a Christmas tree effect.*

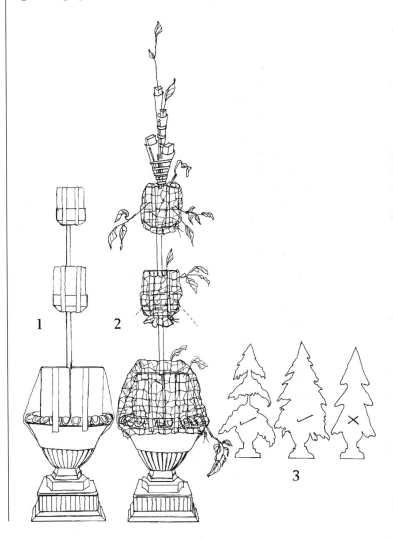

are some very good stands to hold buckets upright and firm and these are well worth buying if much flower decoration in the future is envisaged. Slopped water and fallen buckets with damaged contents are a nuisance.

So to the church, and try not to be late. Aim to be there at least half an hour beforehand, and delegate a job for each helper, with everyone detailed to bring in the flowers and foliages. A large sheet of plastic on which to stand the buckets and flower and foliage boxes will save a lot of clearing-up time at the end.

Allocate the flowers to be used for the arrangements and ensure that the arrangers have foliages suited to their designs. In the excitement to get going, it is very easy to take special pieces, such as long ivy trails, that are then cut into short lengths for a small design. Indicating the foliages to be used is preferable and also ensures that the designs all have a fair selection of flowers. While it is only natural that each arranger will want her design to look especially good, this is a team effort and needs a good overall appearance, not one stunning and two thin designs.

OPPOSITE *The designs are placed on either side of the altar, with the two smaller arrangements placed at the altar rail.*

As the arrangements are being worked, it is a good idea to walk round and see how things are progressing. If the design is not how you envisaged, then say so at this stage. It will be too late to get it changed once it is finished.

Stop for a break and time to assess the progress that has been made. The coffee and tea will be very welcome and a good time for mutual admiration of the arrangements. It is always good to stand back or get away from designs for a short while. On returning, either the 'holes' will be obvious or the design will look very much better than was anticipated.

Clearing Up

When all is completed, it is time to clear up. This is as important as the arranging and needs to be done well. Dropped leaves or petals give an immediate impression of dying flowers, however fresh they might really be. Mopping up any spills or marks is best done as they happen, but is not always possible. Wooden table tops must be wiped and if necessary polished a little to avoid water stains. A top-up with water, a final spray and all is complete: the church a delight with wedding decoration.

The same process now needs to be repeated for the reception, and then, when completed, it's home to work on the bouquets and posies.

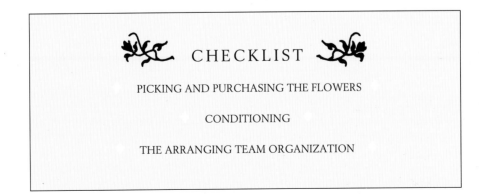

CHECKLIST

PICKING AND PURCHASING THE FLOWERS

CONDITIONING

THE ARRANGING TEAM ORGANIZATION

5

FLOWERS FOR THE BRIDAL PARTY

THE BOUQUETS, HEADDRESSES, posies, buttonholes and other designs that the bridal party will need are most important; they are very much a part of the dress design and the colour scheme. Silk flowers are becoming more and more popular, but for me they will never quite take the place of the 'real thing'. The reason for using silk flowers becomes obvious once you start making bouquets and so on with fresh flowers: they must be very carefully conditioned to stay fresh and also well worked to stay in place. Dead flowers happily dropping petals and flopping over during the service are not to be recommended!

Floristry

Floristry is a very skilled art and for the most part I leave it to the experts. However, people often prefer to work this part of their plans 'in house', and with this in mind I show several designs that are relatively easy to manage. It is often the simplest ideas that seem to be the most complicated, and it is a good idea to practise working the proposed designs well ahead of time. There is no time for experimenting on the night before or on the day of the wedding.

Although easily worked, the designs shown are time-consuming and it is no good expecting to be able to throw the posy or buttonhole together at the last moment. For floristry to look right, it has to be made quietly and in a composed, orderly way. (Perhaps this is why I find it so difficult!)

The bride will already have chosen her designs. The decision will not have been easy to make with so many styles from which to choose – such as a very beautiful full-blown shower. This is a delight, but not for the inexperienced arranger. A tied posy is a very attractive idea and suits so many of the simple wedding dresses and bridesmaids of all ages. This has been illustrated and can of course use a very wide range of materials. Even though the design looks very simple, it must be carefully assembled, to keep it together – young bridesmaids often have a tendency to get excited and twiddle and twirl both themselves and their posies.

A Sheaf

A sheaf of flowers is a lovely idea and can look stunning simply with lilies or roses. A similar but fuller design with garden flowers and trailing ivies is equally beautiful. The design, of course, depends on the dress and style of wedding. If a sheaf is chosen, then I would suggest that the bride or bridesmaid is given a brief note on the best way to hold it. It should be placed so that it

OPPOSITE *A tied posy has been placed on the buffet table in the marquee and, as can be seen, stands very well.*

WIRING FLOWERS AND FOLIAGES

The three illustrations of wiring are fairly typical of most of the materials that will be needed.

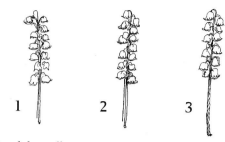

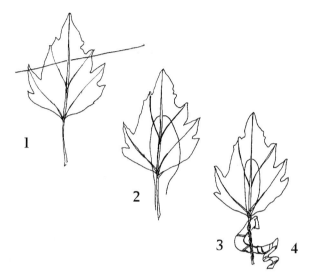

Lily-of-the-valley
1. *Make a small hook at the end of a fine wire. Hook it over near the top of the stem and keep the wire parallel to it.*
2. *Very carefully twist the wire between the bells and then pull the remainder down the stem.*
3. *Bind very firmly with stem tape.*

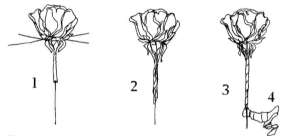

Ivy
1. *Thread a fine wire through the back of the ivy leaf, about half-way down, making a 'stitch`.*
2. *Bend the wires down to give equal lengths.*
3. *Wind one wire around the stem and the other.*
4. *Tape the stem with floral tape.*

Rose
1. *Insert a wire into the stem end.*
2. *Thread a fine wire through the base of the rose in each direction.*
3. *Bring the wires down to the stem and wire together.*
4. *Tape the stem with floral tape.*

can rest very comfortably on the arm, with the hand gently over the stem ends . . . not, as I have seen, held very inelegantly in the hand with the flowers stuck up in the air. As the sheaf has a long, stylish shape, it does need support or the flowers will easily damage.

A Posy

A wired posy or bouquet is very pretty and fairly simple to make for a flower arranger who has had some previous experience of wiring and taping flowers. If new to arranging flowers, I would suggest either a lot of practice well ahead of time or perhaps a course in floristry if this is really what is wanted. For those who would like to make a design with simple wiring, the illustrations show the basic method. This can easily be adapted to suit most types of design, including buttonholes, corsages, muffs, bonnets and hats. With bonnets, muffs and hats I would suggest that the wired designs are then stitched on to or into them.

For those who just cannot master fine wiring and taping, there is help at hand in the shape of a posy-holder. This is a gadget which can be purchased from a florist or garden store; it has a small plastic handle and a piece of floral foam set into it in which to place the flowers. A very pretty posy design can be worked, almost as if making an arrangement. If the design required

The flowers for the headdress and wreath are wired as shown and then taped on to a basic wire which has a hook and loop for fastening. Handle the flowers as little as possible to avoid damage to the petals.

is to be more in the shape of a spray, I feel that it is a good idea to wire the longer pieces well into the back of the holder.

Basket Designs

Basket designs are very suitable for wedding flowers and are probably the best arrangement for a novice to tackle. The shape of the basket is important. It should be light and comfortable to carry. There are so many lovely styles of baskets that it is well worth taking a little time to

A TIED POSY

1. *Condition materials well.*
2. *Cross the first two stems as shown.*
3. *Continue to add the stems in the same way.*
4. *Build up the design until all the stems are employed.*
5. *Bind the stems together. Trim the stem ends level (Take care, however, not to work too industriously or you could end up with no stalks at all!)*
6. *Knot the stems securely.*
7. *Add a double ribbon bow to complete the design.*

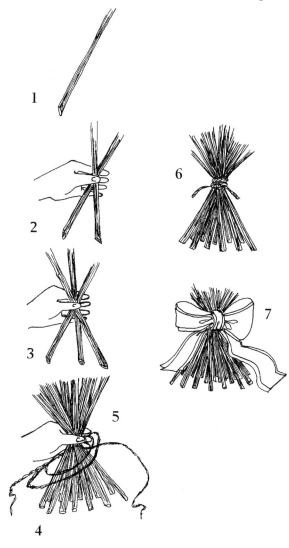

have a good look before making a final decision. The old traditional 'picking basket' is perfect for a summer bride, with lovely soft garden flowers and foliages, and there are also some very good baskets with one flat side and one shaped that allow a very elegant flowing design to be worked. (Not unlike the design worked for the tall pillars.) Use well-drained floral foam, wrapped in fine plastic to prevent the water dripping or seeping. The fine plastic will need to be well covered with foliages and flowers as it does have a very unhappy knack of glistening in the sun or flash lights, one or both of which is bound to be in evidence during the day. Although pushing the stems well into the foam is not a good idea when arranging normally, it does help to press a few down well and so cause crossing of some of them below the surface; this will help to wedge the design firmly. A warning, though: do not pull the flowers or foliages out to rework them or you will damage the foam; if it is necessary to change one or two pieces, cut them out and rearrange as desired.

Simplicity Itself

Perhaps the simplest of all designs is just to have one flower – the idea started by a notable Royal many years ago – but the single flower must be beautiful and held well, unless it is to look like an afterthought! One very beautiful rose or a longiflorum lily would be perfect.

Designs for Small Attendants

Designs for small bridesmaids or pages are often difficult to choose. Excitement and over-tiredness tend to cause some difficulties and easy-to-hold or easy-to-wear ideas are often very much better. Hoops are lovely, as made popular by a Royal some time ago. Garlands, which are very good at keeping everyone

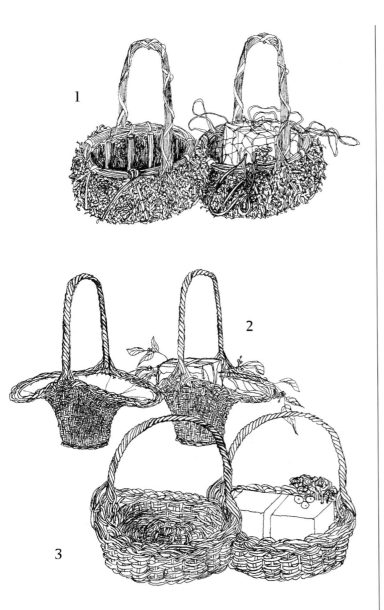

together, are also beautiful. Winter weddings can have such delights as muffs and bonnets (very pretty to carry or to wear) and small hanging purses are practical. For flower girls, decorated baskets are lovely. Make sure, when choosing a basket for the very small, that it will stand firmly without toppling over.

Getting Designs to the Bridal Party in Perfect Condition

All these designs have to be worked at the last moment and will need to be taken to the home of the bride and to the bridal party. Transporting

BASKET DESIGNS

The illustrations above show some of the many types of baskets that can be used and some simple mechanics and designs to use in them.
1. Woven design in a mossed basket.
2. Traditional arrangement in a prettily shaped design.
3. A design with blocked colour and a flat or cut-off finished appearance.

BASKETS FOR FLOWER GIRLS

1. A covered design.
2. A garland decorating the edge.

them is very important and does require a little planning ahead to ensure that everything is in pristine condition when it arrives. A good-sized box is useful; one of the flower boxes would be excellent, with tissue paper crumpled into it. Place the designs carefully into the box, avoiding touching them as much as possible. Any very heavy materials will need a little support, and extra crumpled tissue paper will help here. Ribbon bows also benefit from a little tissue paper tucked into them to prevent them from being flattened. If the weather is warm, a very fine spray of water will help to keep the designs fresh. Then it's another layer of tissue paper over the whole lot and the lid placed on the top, with a large notice saying '*This Side Up*'!

The mossed basket holds rosebuds and violets packed tightly into damp foam. The basket has been lined with fine clear plastic to prevent any leakage. A gardenia buttonhole is also shown with a Victorian posy holder containing a pretty design of rosebuds, violets and lily-of-the-valley.

Extra Help for Very Delicate Designs

If the journey is considerable, very delicate designs can be stitched into the box, but do put on a notice to say so or they will be wrenched apart by the enthusiastic recipient, which could be a disaster. One last word about the journey: keep the boxes as cool as possible; never leave them on the shelf at the back of the car in the hot sun or you will have cooked the contents!

Preserving the Wedding Bouquets

One lovely idea that can be thought about is keeping the bouquet after the wedding. There are several ways in which this can be managed, either with silica gel or by pressing the materials individually. There are many advertisements for preserving bouquets in bride magazines, but it is necessary to organize this before the wedding, so that it can be worked on as soon as possible after the celebrations. It is not very easy to preserve a beautiful posy if it is half dead! To preserve the posy yourself is possible but quite time-consuming. Perhaps removing just one or two flowers to press would be more practical.

RIGHT *The bonnet and muff have been decorated with delicate, pretty flowers which were bound on to a very fine wire with white tape, and then carefully stitched in position.*

CHECKLIST

CHOICE OF DESIGN

TRAVELLING WITH FLOWERS

PRESERVING THE DESIGNS

6

*F*LOWER DESIGNS FOR THE MARRIAGE CEREMONY

CREATING THE DECORATIONS for a marriage is always a joy, whether for a simple or a grand occasion. Every service is unique, with the style and the choice of colouring special to the bride, fulfilling her many plans and dreams. The right flowers will create an atmosphere as nothing else can and will bring a feeling of well-being to the celebration.

To show as many as possible of the decorative ideas that can be used for the marriage service, the arrangements have been designed to cover a variety of needs and also to suggest, with the sketches, other possibilities. The archway is a typical example of this, in that it can be used in a garden, a tent, a porch or a screen, adapted as required. Swags and garlands are also marvellous decorations that can be used in many situations.

Budgets

The budget will inevitably be the deciding factor on the number and types of flowers to be used. Important as it is, though, with good planning limited finance need not mean just one very skimped pedestal design. There are many inexpensive and attractive ideas that can be used. If finance is of no consequence, then a word of warning here is important: do not overwhelm with extravagant and oversized designs. You will be in a place of worship and

the building should still be visible. Enhancing is the key word and the decorations should be elegantly and tastefully worked, setting the scene for the service without giving the feeling of a flower festival or perhaps trying to convey an impression of wealth. Flowers are never pompous and certainly look more than uncomfortable if they are used in this way.

Focal Points

The most important design for the service is the one where the marriage will be performed, and the design or designs should be placed near to where the bride and groom will be standing together. It is good to create a focal point, but also to remember to keep the designs in proportion. Do not be tempted to surround the couple in a bower of flowers which will hide them and the altar from the congregation. If, as with arranging flowers in church for other occasions, it is remembered that the altar is the most important part of the place of worship, then it will be simplicity itself to avoid the pitfall of over-enthusiasm.

The altar is a lovely position for flowers, if they are allowed, but large or heavy designs will not be right. A few lilies carefully placed will be far more in keeping than an oversized arrangement. Making a few rough sketches of the areas that are to be decorated is always a good idea (no need to be a skilled artist).

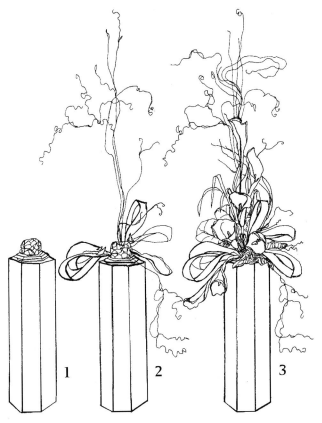

MODERN DESIGN

A modern design arranged in a very modern church with pillars that have been painted to give a polished-stone effect.
1. A container following the hexagonal shape of the pillars has floral foam and wire netting securely fixed for the mechanics.
2. The outline is created with contorted willow. Aspidistra leaves are wound back on themselves and the stem pushed gently through the leaf to give the ribbon shape.
3. Arum lilies, leaves and twigs are added to complete the design.

Shading in the approximate size of the proposed arrangements will help to determine the best size and the number needed. Understatement is always far more elegant than its opposite.

I prefer, if possible, the designs where the bride and groom are to stand to frame them;

this does mean, however, that two or more designs will be required. Budget-conscious arrangers can always use the same number of flowers and supplement the shortfall with good foliages, berries and blossoms. In fact, I prefer arrangements with these materials to those exclusively of massed flowers. Pedestals, tall candlesticks, pillars and urns are all good for such positions.

Pew End and Pillar Designs

Pew end designs are lovely and add a sparkle throughout the entire church, but not for every pew; using alternate or every third row is preferable (you can have too much of a good thing!). The illustrations shows many mechanics and methods that can be used, and all are simple to work, especially a small basket that could just have a pot plant of primroses placed in it. Trailing pieces of pretty ivies always add a natural touch to the design and, for me, replace the ribbons so often used. If ribbons are to be used, avoid the shiny type, which are better suited to the reception festivities, and use instead the paper ribbon string which, when unwound, gives a lovely, soft and easily managed bow with the appearance of wild silk. Of course, wild silk is marvellous, especially if it is what is used in the dresses of the bride or her attendants. If the fabrics from the dresses are available, try using those of both the bride and her attendants together . . . just beautiful.

Pillars are a delight to decorate and the illustrations show several ideas that can be used. Again, it is important to decide how much is to be decorated as although pew ends and pillars are lovely, they will fight for your attention and might cancel each other out. Choose the position that is best suited to the size and style of the building. Pillar decorations will require a considerable amount of material and this could be a factor in deciding between one and the other. Of course, if the building is very large, both could well be needed. Again, the illustrations show several ways in which they can be decorated, with the mechanics required.

Windowsills and Fonts

Windowsills are another lovely area to decorate, especially in a small building where space is limited. The main difficulty with this type of decoration is the light which floods in, making

The elegance of the modern design suits the setting admirably and the arrangements in front of the altar echo the idea, creating a stunning simplicity and delightful setting for the modern young bride.

it quite difficult to create a good arrangement that does not have the appearance of only stalks. Large leaves placed at the back of the arrangement help, and using fairly large flowers in the centre of the design can also improve the appearance. A good window arrangement is a delight, but one filled with light is a sight!

A window design for a winter wedding will not have the very bright sunlight to contend with, but another problem can arise with dark foliages set against a dreary sky. This can be greatly improved with the addition of candles and/or variegated foliages. White flowers, although easily seen, will create a very chilly feeling. Introducing those with just a warm flush of the palest peach or pink will look absolutely marvellous.

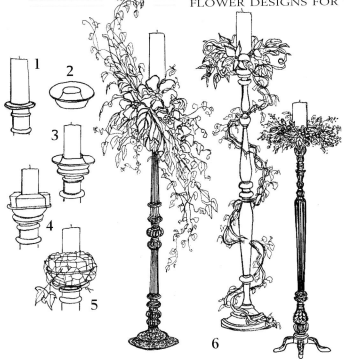

ALTAR DESIGNS IN CANDLESTICKS

1. *The candle is placed in the candleholder.*
2. *A Baba or rice mould.*
3. *The mould placed over the candlestick.*
4. *Foam blocks placed in the mould.*
5. *Wire netting secured with wire is placed over the whole.*
6. *Designs that can be worked with these mechanics.*

BELOW *The delightful use of the moulds shows how elegant a design can be using such simple mechanics. Here the lilies have been allowed to frame the altar and show to great advantage the very beautiful candlesticks.*

Many places of worship have especially attractive areas to arrange flowers, but few can be lovelier than a font. In the illustration three ways to decorate them are shown, but it is important – as with all your chosen sites for flowers – to obtain permission for their use. There may well be a ban against using the font as a container, but no problem if just the rim or ledge is decorated.

A canopy in a synagogue is also a joy when decorated for the ceremony (the design shown on the roof of the garden pavilion is a lovely idea that can be employed here).

Many churches have removed the screens that separated the chancel from the nave, but where they do remain they are a very lovely site for decorations, garlands and swags being particularly suitable.

Making an Entrance

I especially love to see flowers in the porch or entrance, to give a welcome to the guests as they arrive and to set the scene. The colour scheme, if there is one, and the style of the day can be happily conveyed in this way. The gateway, or lych gate, is also good to decorate, creating a very attractive setting for photographs. This certainly tells the world at large that there is a wedding going on.

The following is a list of suitable positions for flowers, but remember that although all of them can look marvellous when decorated, it is important to decide on the amount that will look best in each case. Select carefully the best sites and stay with it. Do not be tempted to 'do' another here and another there, or the

OPPOSITE *The pew end and pillar designs have been made using wall baskets. The baskets have been lined with plastic before having floral foam taped and wired into them. The foliages are allowed to trail from the baskets, giving a very relaxed and happy feeling.*

PEW ENDS

Mechanics and ideas that can be used for pew ends.

1A. *Plastic tray.*
1B. *Plastic tray prepared for use with soaked floral foam and held in position with floral tape.*
2. *Foam tray containing foam ready to be soaked.*
3. *'Le clip', a pew end device that is fully adjustable.*
4. *Heavier-style pew end with solid handle.*
5. *Cheeseboard with foam covered in plastic and taped in position.*
6. *Pottery wall container.*
7. *Wire-work wall container.*
8A. *Wall basket.*
8B. *Mechanics suitable for wall basket (NB Provision must be made to line the basket).*
9. *Plastic-covered wire plant basket.*
10. *Plastic plant holder.*
11. *Cornucopia. Check for lining.*

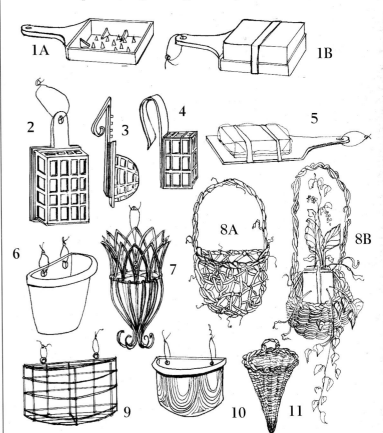

FONT DESIGNS

1. The mechanics required for creating an arrangement on the ledge of the font. Flat plastic trays with floral foam have been taped securely. Ensure that the tape to be used is easily removed and will not mark the wood-work or stonework in any way. A simple but interest-ing design is needed, using very pretty and unusual materials, keeping the shape neat and not overly large. Interwoven stems could look very good here.

2. The mechanics required for creating an arrange-ment within the font. A liner of some kind is necessary and a plastic washing-up bowl is ideal. Floral foam well taped and wire-netted in position is good; as an alternative crumpled wire netting securely wired in place is equally effective. With the latter, it is impor-tant to keep the water level well up to ensure that all the materials stay fresh. It is necessary to check that there are no leaves rotting away in the water as this can create a very unpleasant odour. (This will not help to ensure the best atmosphere!)

3. The mechanics required to make an arrangement on the side of a font. Foam packs have been wired securely to the side of the font and can be easily worked. This style of design is good if free-flowing and soft in appearance, avoiding the pitfall of a stodgy design by recessing some of the materials.

result will be a muddle and uncomfortable on the eye. Well-placed, restrained and beautiful designs are the order of the day . . . leave the riot of colour and excitement for the reception.

Lych gates	Pew ends
Porches	Choir stalls
Fonts	Altars
Windowsills	Canopies
Lecterns	Doorways
Pulpits	Doors
Pillars	Screens

Position of bride and groom

Table where the Register is signed

Position of soloist (if there is to be one)

Rear door for departure

Harmony of the Design

Having suggested various positions for arrange-ments and also, hopefully, some useful tips, it is a good idea to get on with the arrangements. The illustrations will help with the mechanics and ideas for them. Each design made has been planned as a whole, and not just to show a sin-gle type of design that bears no relation to any other. Just as the plans have been coordinated to give a sense of harmony, atmosphere and pleasure to the eye, so too the flowers here have been planned to create an overall and an

OPPOSITE *The font has been decorated with soft autumnal colourings. The height of the design is not overpowering and the foliages flow down softly to create a very elegant appearance.*

TWISTED TREE DESIGNS

1. The branches have been chosen carefully and trimmed a little to enable them to be set into a quick-setting cement base. (A piece of plastic inside the mould for the cement will enable easy removal.) The top branches have been trimmed to receive a piece of wood, which is then nailed into them.

2. A tray containing floral foam is placed on the wood and securely wired in position. The cement base is placed in an attractive pot.

3. The design is created, allowing the foliages to flow down well. Hydrangeas, chrysanthemums, dahlias and carnations have been used, with interesting foliages and wheat. Fruits and berries would look particularly attractive also.

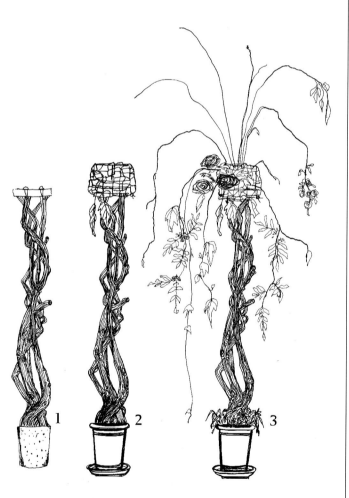

integrated feeling. There are designs for all seasons, which of course can be adapted for different times simply by using other foliages and flowers. Adapting the arrangements to suit the situation is the aim, and with this in mind it should be easier to transpose the idea, for example, of a spring garland to one for winter, or a font design from autumn to summer. The basic requirements are the correct mechanics; the types of flowers and foliages used will be those of the appropriate season.

The Lych Gate

The lych gate is sometimes a problem in that inclement weather may well just demolish the arrangement if it is not sturdy enough. Whatever the colour scheme and type of flowers to be used, the gate does have some special needs all of its own. The mechanics will have to be well anchored down and well hidden, as the arrangements here will be viewed at very close quarters. As with the basket designs, the foam will have to be wrapped in thin plastic to avoid drying out and to prevent drips falling on to the guests below.

Stout wire is needed but not nails. The appearance of the gate is important to the wedding, but so is the condition of the gate when all have departed. (Wire is perhaps more fiddly to put up, but much quicker to take down afterwards – always good to remember.)

OPPOSITE *The twisted trees have been made to decorate the porch and also the inner porch. (Two in the one area would have been a little overwhelming unless the designs were smaller.) Autumn foliages such as abelia and stephanandra add to the colour and soft flowing style of the design. This type of arrangement would look equally lovely at any time of the year.*

Trays with handles, sometimes called funeral trays or frying pans, are very useful for this type of design and, as the illustrations show, can be used in many different ways. Blocks of foam wrapped in wire netting are equally good, and again it is wise to wrap the foam or tray in thin plastic. They should all be well soaked and then allowed to drain a little, ensuring that the foam is wet throughout, especially in the middle.

If necessary, a frame can be made to take the trays, but usually with this particular design there are more than enough spots to use for the arrangements. The design for gates needs to be bold, but not necessarily large, and certainly not so large that the guests have difficulty getting through without being impaled or caught up on the flowers and foliages. Hardy flowers are needed. Materials such as carnations, chrysanthemums and the all-year-round chrysanthemums will survive in most types of weather, from the hottest to the wettest. Ivy and *Rubus tricolor* are good for trailing pieces, and if materials such as Old man's beard, fatsias or beech that have been glycerined are used they will look wonderful.

Do not be tempted to smother the gate – most lych gates are very attractive – but look for the best positions for the flowers, such as those that will give a festive feeling and add to the gate's appearance. Here the colour scheme can be revealed and will help to create the wedding atmosphere for all those who pass by or through.

Gates other than lych gates are also fun to decorate; swags, garlands and plaques look particularly good. Initials of the happy couple picked out in flower heads create a very personal touch. These can be very easily worked in floral foam and, if necessary, can be made several days ahead of the wedding day. A light spray will normally be enough to keep everything in good order.

Porches

Porches are again a good area to decorate. Even if they are very small, a touch of colour adds greatly to the atmosphere. Flat plastic trays or dishes containing floral foam are simplicity itself to use and far better than a pottery vase or jug, which could easily be knocked over. Unless the porch is very spacious, like the one illustrated, small designs are much better, as the number of people passing to and fro makes it at times a very congested area. If there is plenty of space, then this is an ideal position for a more unusual or special design. A pedestal design should include unusual materials and be of a style that includes trailing ivies or suchlike as the whole of it will be seen.

Topiary for Unusual Designs

The twisted trees that have been made are a very good decorative idea and are easily worked for all seasons. Simple topiary of the bay-tree type is another suggestion, although again the design will be more interesting if there are some pieces of foliage allowed to trail down almost to the container. (Even a textured trunk is preferable to a smooth broom-handle painted brown or covered with shiny ribbon; the addition of some thin twigs intertwined with the trunk will greatly improve the design.) Here again I prefer to use dull ribbons or the ribbon string, feeling that they are more in keeping with the situation, rather than the very shiny types, which can be reserved for the reception.

Topiary and obelisks are great fun to use and marvellous subjects for porch decorations, especially because they can be made well ahead of time.

Archways

An archway of foliages and flowers, either on the inner or the outer door-frame, is a joy and also creates a marvellous setting for photographs. The archway can use a multitude of materials and need not necessarily be costly. In spring catkins and pussy willow will look very good, and in early summer cow parsley and marguerites are a delight; for autumn or winter designs foliages, either fresh or glycerined with berries and fruits, will be just stunning.

A simple frame will be needed for the archway and this can be easily purchased from a garden store in either plastic-coated wire or wood. A handyman could make such a frame quite easily, and I would suggest, if this can be done, making it in sections for easy transportation. (It will surprise you how often the frame is used and also how often people ask to borrow such a mechanic.)

Pot-et-Fleur with Flair

Pot-et-fleur designs are another very useful decoration for the porch and can also be arranged well ahead of the wedding day, with just the fresh flowers added at the time of arranging. Certainly this type of design is both a good focal point and a good talking point! (Pot-et-fleur should be used more than they are. The initial cost of the plants is very quickly absorbed by the high cost of flowers that would have been purchased week by week.)

The font is usually well placed and therefore marvellous for decorations, if they are allowed. Sometimes only the rim or sides are permitted to be decorated. Whatever the designs, a font will be 'good value for money' and a delight to the eye. If the bowl of the font is to be used, it must have a liner placed in it. (A plastic washing-up bowl or something similar is ideal.) Floral foam and wire netting with water are both equally good for mechanics. If the rim or sides are to be decorated, floral foam packs are useful. Remember that the font is used for christenings and designs here are lovely if

ARCHWAY DESIGNS

1. *Floral foam packs attached to the metal support allow a very attractive design to be created. Allow trailing pieces to hang well down and to intertwine with the archway support to give a feeling of organic growth.*
2. *A floral foam tray wired to a pillar.*
3. *A framework attached to the archway with floral foam packs for the flowers. Here a filled-in design works very well and is highly decorative.*

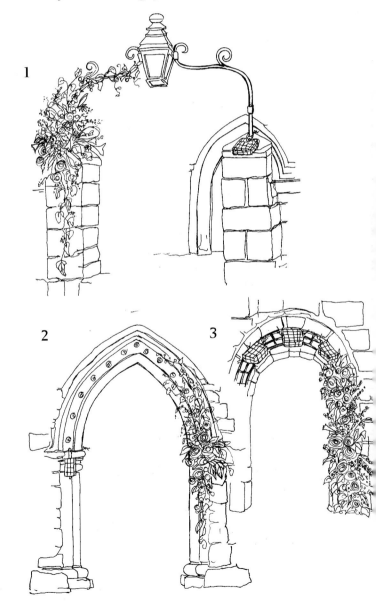

57

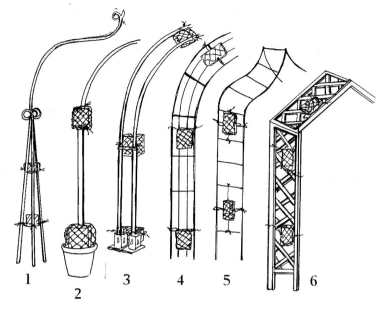

1 2 3 4 5 6

VARIOUS METHODS OF MAKING ARCHWAYS

1. *Purchased wrought-iron frame.*
2. *Basic tree mechanics with fine plastic piping for the arch.*
3. *Fence support bases with plastic piping set into them, with cement and finer piping to make the archway.*
4. *Frame in either wood or plastic-covered wire.*
5. *One of many designs in metalwork that can be purchased.*
6. *Trellis archway, which can be purchased in many styles or made by a handy person.*

All the styles of archway will need foam packs wired to them for the flowers and foliages. Always wrap the foam in fine plastic first, to prevent excessive loss of water.

allowed to remind the guests of this fact. An overpowering, heavy and brightly coloured design will not really feel quite right, even though it does follow the colour scheme. Far better to echo the colouring in softer shades and tones – very elegant and adding yet another dimension to the atmosphere. The illustrations show several ways in which to create attractive designs for a font.

Pillars

Pillar decorations are a delight and have the advantage of being easily seen. However, the mechanics for such areas are sometimes quite difficult and it is vital that no nails or screws are used. (Sometimes one can be found in a convenient place, but this cannot be relied upon.) Wire and stout string are relatively easy to manage and much better for the fabric of the building.

The pillar designs are just a few of many that can be worked; some of the Victorian flower books for church decoration are a good source of ideas. Again, it is important to keep within the bounds of wedding decorations and not those of a flower festival. It is easy to get carried away with the idea of fountains of flowers sweeping down to the guests, but this is not very practical nor in the right spirit of a service.

The altar in every place of worship is important, and as such requires care in the decoration. Not all ministers will allow the altar to be decorated with flowers and permission must be gained first before sallying forth. Elegant simplicity is, I feel, the name of the game here, and I certainly do not like to see the altar swamped with arrangements. A few simple lilies will speak volumes.

OPPOSITE *A frame has been used to create the archway arrangement. The foliages were not used only to cover the mechanics, but also to help give an elegant feeling to the design, by allowing some trailing pieces gently to break the outline.*

Although the flowers and foliages are allowed to flow over the top of the doorway, they are swept back at the sides to avoid impeding the guests as they enter or leave. This will also, of course, prevent any damage to the flowers.

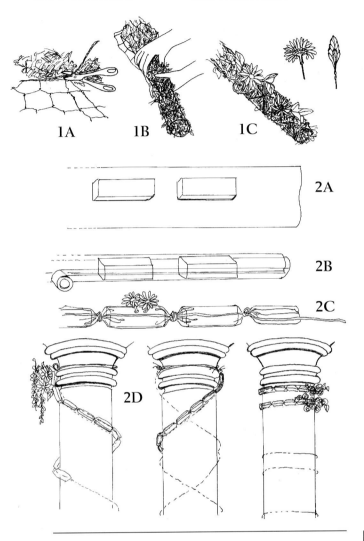

1A   1B   1C

2A

2B

2C

2D

GARLANDS

Mossed garlands. Mechanics needed: sphagnum moss, wire netting, flowers and foliages (wired if necessary).
1A. *Trim away the thick edging of the netting and cut a strip about 9 inches wide and 36 inches long.*
1B. *Place the sphagnum moss along the centre of the wire netting and roll the netting around the moss, using the cut ends of the netting to secure the roll together. Press the roll gently to give one slightly flatter side.*
1C *Wired flowers and foliages are pushed into the moss.*

Foam 'sausages'. Mechanics needed: floral foam cut into neat shapes (one foam block is suitable for approximately eight smaller blocks), fine plastic sheeting (the plastic used by dry cleaners is perfect), string and clear tape.
2A. *Cut the plastic into pieces approximately 9 inches by 36 inches (I find this particular length the most manageable). Lay the sausage shapes along the length of the plastic, spacing them carefully (nine or ten usually fit in comfortably). Allow a reasonable amount over at either end; this will have to be tied to the next length if a longer garland is required.*
2B. *Fold the plastic over and seal with the clear tape.*
2C. *With the string, tie along the length of the garland and make an extra knot between each sausage. Leave long pieces of string at either end for attaching or joining.*
2D. *How garlands can be used for pillars.*

OPPOSITE *Trailing garlands for summer: floral foam sausages have been wound round and down the pillar to create this summer design.*

It is important to cover the plastic well as it does have an irritating habit of glistening through the design. Small bunches of foliage can help to fill the background more easily and quickly.

If you seem to be having difficulty piercing the plastic with some of the finer materials, use a small toothpick or something similar to puncture a hole through which the stem can be pushed. Do not make the hole too large or the stem will not be held firmly in the foam and will fall out. It is sensible to allocate the flowers evenly throughout the whole length of the garland or you will find it very full at the beginning and very sparse at the end!

The mechanics illustrated in this diagram are easily made and, of course, very inexpensive, but they are time-consuming. If a great deal of garlanding is planned, then it could well be worth while buying some lay-flat plastic tubing. This has to be purchased in commercial lengths, although there is a small user length of about 500 feet. Lay-flat tubing is made in many widths, from 2 inches upwards. Using the tubing will involve simply cutting to the required length, feeding in damp floral foam sausage shapes and twisting or tying as necessary. I feel that this is the finest tubing for the garland making, but it will involve stringing to keep it secure, especially for the heavier designs.

HOOP DESIGN

A purchased hoop of twisted vine has been decorated with a wired garland of flowers and pretty foliages.

If difficult flowers have been chosen, then the small orchid tubes can be used; with the flowers safely installed and in water, they can be carefully wired into the design.

LEFT *A hoop of twisted vine is propped up against a pew end that has been decorated with similar flowers in a moss-lined vine basket. Wired ribbon has been added to the designs.*

An arrangement can also be seen on the windowsill with the foliage allowed to flow over the edge, creating an easy and natural design that coordinates well with the pew end arrangement.

Altar Flowers

Arrangements on either side of the altar are lovely and do frame the bride and groom beautifully, bringing the whole together. Identical designs are not as lovely as two that complement each other – that is, the same shape but with a slight variation to add interest. Containers other than the overly used wrought-iron pedestal are good, and some suggestions for these can be found in the chapter on receptions (flowers for a village hall). They can add a distinctive touch to the arrangements.

Choir stalls and lecterns look lovely when decorated quite simply with garlands, and these can be made well ahead of time and draped and tied in position on the day.

Making an Exit

Leaving after the service is sometimes a lengthy process and a little thought to the appearance of the arrangements that will be re-viewed on the way out is a good idea. Certainly the guests will be seeing the flowers from a fresh angle and will be able to look at them more closely, with the time to enjoy the designs and the particular materials that have been used. I have always liked the idea of ensuring that the flowers have been arranged with the vicar in mind, making the backs of the arrangements as attractive as the fronts (well nearly, anyway!). If this is remembered it will be easy to create arrangements to look beautiful from every angle.

If there is a balcony or gallery, garlands and swags look very attractive and give a lovely visual appeal as the bridal party and the guests depart.

The Photography

The photography of the bride and groom, the attendants, the parents and friends is then the order of the day, and gives time for everyone to meet, chat and admire. The bridal party will be clearly the centre of attention and the floristry very much in evidence. If an archway of flowers has been made it will provide a lovely setting for photographs. With the photography completed, it is then time for the happy couple and their guests to be whisked away to the reception amidst a shower of rose petals.

CHECKLIST

FOCAL POINTS TO BE DECORATED

IMPORTANCE OF HARMONY IN THE ARRANGEMENT

SPECIAL DESIGNS FOR SPECIAL AREAS

PHOTOGRAPHIC CONSIDERATIONS

7

INSPIRATION AND IDEAS FOR FLOWERS FOR THE RECEPTION

THE HOME OF THE BRIDE is still considered the most suitable place to hold the wedding reception, and this is perhaps one of the best traditions that has survived throughout the many generations of wedding feasts. Fortunately, it is not now the custom to involve the whole village, although this must have been great fun. However, a reception at home does have the special bonus of friendly faces and familiar surroundings, although it is very hard work for all the family.

The most important point to remember with decorations for the home is that, with pre-wedding nerves and many people around, the organization for the flowers must be well planned, with all the mechanics fully prepared. The bride's mother will not want to be finding wire or containers for you at the last moment, or discover foam being soaked in the freshly cleaned cloakroom. Take everything, including your own coffee and biscuits, and work invisibly!

The Problem of Space

If the home is very large, then space will not be a problem, but even with the most expansive area, there never seems to be quite enough room. This is where a tent, marquee or plastic awning can work wonders.

A summer wedding is usually the most suitable one for a reception in the garden and can be a delight, but wherever you are weather conditions will demand a canopy or cover of some type, be it as protection against the odd shower, a downpour or the sun. Simple plastic-sheeting cover, from the walls of the house and just supported on slim poles with guy ropes, is marvellous for adding another entertaining area for the guests. This simple device will offer shade and space for seating for small tables and chairs. This type of protection will not of course be adequate for gale-force winds or frosty, wintry conditions, but is ideal to use in warm spring through to autumn days. Small tables can be prettily decorated with cloths, paper if preferred (well anchored down), and small flower arrangements or pots of plants. A very effective and simple decoration can be worked using terracotta pots from the greenhouse with bright geranium plants in zingy colourings. Further pots of plants can be added if desired to create a very attractive setting. If the plastic sheeting is a little drab, draping striped or any soft fabric over it will give a very elegant air, and using a mosquito net or netting as a lining gives a soft, romantic feeling to the otherwise plain plastic surface.

Summer weddings at home will invariably stretch well into the evening and coloured

WHITE GARDEN PAVILION

1. *A basic method of mechanics for an arrangement, using floral foam and floral foam tape to keep the foam in place. If it is felt to be necessary, a pinholder or foamholder can also be used, to keep the floral foam really secure.*

2. *Wire netting has been rolled into a 'Swiss roll' shape and placed into the vase; the centre has to be lifted a little and the netting spaced evenly. String is tied round the top of the vase to hold the netting firmly. If the vase does not have a rim, the string will have to be tied as if for a parcel.*

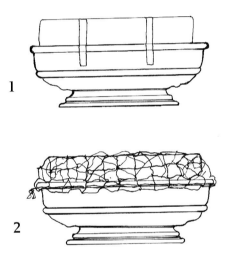

lights and candles can transform the scene. If candles are to be used, then storm glasses are good to counteract the wind (jam jars are equally good), but if electric lights are to be used they must be suitable for outdoors. (An electrician will advise on this if there is any doubt as to safety.) A small walled backyard is just perfect for covering, and if done in this way in the months before the wedding, ivies and plants can be grown in containers on the wall to create a lovely display. There are some very attractive climbing plants that can be grown to make the area more decorative. It is quite easy to find delightful ideas in the proposed colour schemes, but if these are not yet known, it is equally good to grow white flowering varieties.

The perennial sweet pea, White pearl, is very attractive and will be a joy for many years to come, as well as a lovely reminder of a very happy day.

It is easy to see that with a little imagination and perhaps a little toil you will produce the right effect. Roof gardens and terraces can be used in similar ways, or with topiary trees and trelliswork, which could give a delightful appearance. Planning ahead is obviously a cheaper way to decorate the proposed site, but 'instant' plants and trees can often be hired specially for the occasion if the decision to hold the reception at home is a last-minute one. Friends with good pot plants might well be kind enough to loan one or two to help with the cost. Fatsias and fatshederas look very elegant and are robust enough to transport without damage.

OVERLEAF *A small white pavilion has been decorated for a luncheon being held after a Register Office wedding. The inside has garlands arranged with all types of foliages and interesting berries, nuts and hops, to bring a 'garden feel' to the design. The obelisks have been created from a metal frame with blocks of foam covered with wire netting and wired securely in place. Yew has been used for the topiary effect. A piece of the yew is pushed into the foam and then clipped to length; the piece that has been cut off is again pushed into the foam, and the process is repeated until all has been used. (It is very time-consuming to cut all the pieces to the correct length first.)*

The table decoration is stunning, with dramatic and unusual materials. The ornamental cabbages are particularly attractive. The illustrations show two methods that can be used.

The corners of the pavilion have been decorated with long trailing foliages which have been allowed to twist down the guy rope (not just as a decorative measure but also as a good way of warning the guests against falling over it!). The mechanics used are wire-netting cages with floral foam, the latter wrapped in plastic to prevent it drying out too quickly.

The zingy colourings of the wall and table decorations in the marquee have been arranged by blocking the colour; this is very effective for a simple modern style and gives a tailored look to the design.

The table designs have been worked in floral foam rounds and small mirrors have been placed in the centre. This adds another dimension and also makes an attractive effect when small night-lights are placed on them for the evening celebrations. The night-lights should, for safety, be in small glass containers or jars. It is important when candles are used that all sensible precautions are taken.

Tents in Variety

A reception for fifty or so guests can be happily accommodated in a tent that can be hired from a local organization such as the Ranger Guides or Scouts. The tents that are used for their camping expeditions are very good, and far removed from the old-style tents that many will remember from their youth! They often have windows and are probably of frame design, which gives a clear area inside; the canvas will be supported without poles in the centre. Decorating such a tent is relatively easy, and can be as simple or elaborate as the style of wedding dictates. Certainly, with good decorations the tent can be transformed.

As there are no poles to decorate, the side walls and supports offer good areas for designs. However, the supports will not be as stout as those for a more substantial marquee and very heavy designs must be avoided. Garlands are ideal for these situations and can be simple ivy or smilax trails, looped up with ribbons or posies of flowers. The cake and buffet table designs can be arranged to coordinate with the colour scheme. Here again, small tables can be prettily arrayed with matching designs.

The Importance of Making an Entrance

The pathway to the tent from the house looks marvellous with decorations, and acts as a guide for the guests. Small trees are a very

OPPOSITE *The designs for the marquee entrance have been arranged on well-balanced and heavy pillars. The materials used are all very robust and well able to stand light rain and breezes – though not, of course, a force-eight gale. The main design is flanked by pillars with pots containing wire frames with ivies. These have been grown, but a similar idea is easily worked with floral foam balls (available in several sizes).*

attractive idea, and lovely either using foliages alone or with flowers following the wedding colour scheme. Ribbon bows are particularly good tied under the topknot and add a charming touch to the festivities. The new ribbon string is very useful for tree bows, tying elegantly and draping well. If a covered way can be included in the scheme, it is lovely to continue the garland theme in the tent along the sides of the walkway. Combined with the trees, this will provide a vista and a receiving area for the bride and groom.

Ideas for the House

As with all receptions at home, the house will be used by the guests and it is always good to include some arrangements in the house, especially in the cloakroom. The older guests may well prefer to retire to the quiet of the sitting room, and again flowers will be much appreciated there. Unless the colourings of the bridal party are suitable for the decorations in the home, it is preferable to use ones that will tone with the furnishings. Large designs are not really necessary as with many guests they could get in the way or be knocked over. Simple and elegant arrangements will look very special.

Garden Pavilions

For a reception in the garden with perhaps a very few guests, then a simple covered area such as a garden pavilion is a lovely idea. The small tent can be as elegant or as simple as desired. It could, of course, be used as a special area to be married in or for the cake. Decorations on the corners of the roof of flowers and foliages and ivy trails will look splendid and give a very distinctive appearance to perhaps an otherwise very ordinary tent. Decorating the guy ropes is also useful as it draws the guests' attention to the hazard of the rope.

Garlands are perfect for tents and the one that has been photographed just revels in the pretty decor. The garlands are very easily made and inexpensive in materials, but very time-consuming. If garlands are used on the tent, then do not be tempted to garland the table-cloth as well; it will just look too much and become fussily inelegant.

Marquees and Their Needs

With a great number of guests a larger tent or marquee will be required. Marquees come in diverse colours and shapes . . . and I love them all! There are basically two types: one supported by poles and the other by a metal frame. Both are extremely good, and both have advantages and disadvantages - the choice must be yours. The frame tent gives a completely free area inside and often has windows and doors of transparent plastic, allowing one to see into the garden. The alternative does have one or more very tall poles and a considerable number of ropes and stays to keep everything in order. The poles are a joy to decorate and even the guy ropes and stays can be given attractive treatment.

The marquee will have a lining, which can vary in many ways from stripes to rouches and gathers in a plain or striped soft fabric. It is usual to choose a colour to match the colour scheme of the wedding. The little marquee that has been photographed was of a very bright pink and green, and was admirably suited to the evening reception party. The decor of bright zingy pinks looked fantastic in the candlelight, and afterwards for the fireworks. The poles were decorated with swag-style designs, inspired by some seen in a stately home, and the wall decorations echoed the same idea.

The wall lining of the tent is a very important part of the decor and can be as delightfully

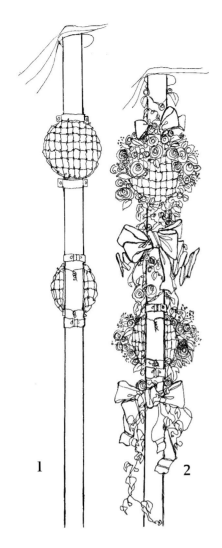

MARQUEE DECORATIONS FOR POLES

Decorating marquee poles is both a challenge and a delight: the possible variations are too many to list them all. Unfortunately, it is often the case that the poles are decorated in a very unimaginative way, with designs far too small. It is surprising how large the designs seem when you are at the top of the pole, but how small when back at ground level. The designs suggested here are all quite easy to manage, as long as a good, tall ladder is available.

1. *Two wire-frame cages containing wet floral foam are clamped to the pole with space between.*
2. *Paper ribbon bows and ivies are plaited around the pole and the flowers arranged in the foam. Long-lasting, dried or silk materials can be used, or a combination of all three, with fresh foliages, as in the design photographed here.*

ABOVE *The gaily coloured marquee has been decorated with long-lasting flowers and ribbon bows. The flowers and foliages have been arranged in foam in wire cages that have been clamped on to the poles, and ribbon string has been plaited through the design and tied into large bows.*

decorated with murals as any French country house. An enterprising artist friend could get the adrenalin going and come up with all sorts of ideas, from an exotic jungle scene to mountains and forests, or an elegant pilastered setting beside the sea, or the Italian lakes . . . what a lovely thought! However, back to practicalities. The marquee chosen will certainly be fun to decorate whatever you choose. Tables, chairs and linen will, of course, be required and these can be borrowed or hired. As an economy I usually use old linen sheets that have been starched to give a fresh appearance. Of course, lovely damask cloths look superb, but I find that by the time the tables are laid and decorated with flowers, the cloth is not noticed, and as the party is in the garden mishaps can occur.

The decorations will have to take into account the particular requirements of the occasion - perhaps the cake table is especially important, or the seating for elderly guests; is there going to be a buffet or a seated meal; what about dancing and the revelries later in the evening? A sketch of the area, taking into account these requirements, will be helpful, and I really do advise planning with a pencil and paper in advance rather than marching round the tent with several people directing the proceedings, all with their own particular views on how the marquee should be arranged. And nor is this the best way to arrange the seating plan!

Contingency Plans

It is important to have a contingency plan for last-minute changes. The marquee erected might just not be the one originally chosen, but with a little forethought your plan can be adaptable to several eventualities. It is also well to be prepared for delays in arrival and for accidents. Things do not always work according to

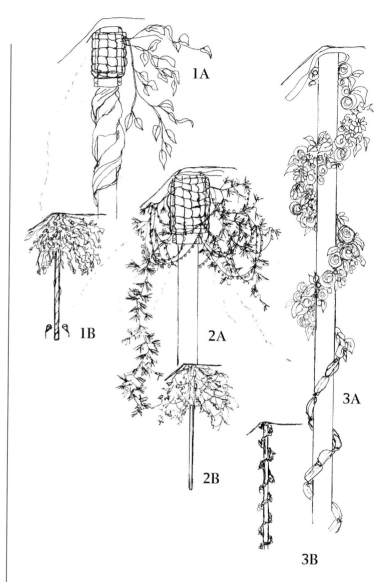

SOME MORE MARQUEE DECORATIONS FOR POLES

1A. *A wire-framed cage, again containing foam, is clamped to the top of the pole and preserved beech has been sprayed with paint.*
1B. *The pole has been draped with paper ribbon and the whole lit from below with spot-lights.*
2A. *Similar mechanics this time employ fir branches, which have been lightly glittered and festooned with tiny Christmas tree lights for a winter wedding.*
2B. *The drawing shows a suitable size for the design.*
3A. *Garlands have been made from the lay-flat tubing and then wound round and down the pole.*
3B. *The design is shown twisting down to the ground.*

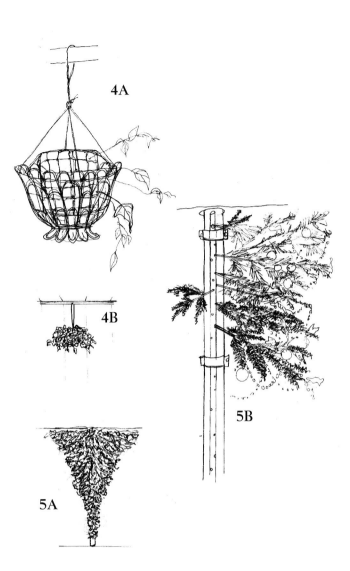

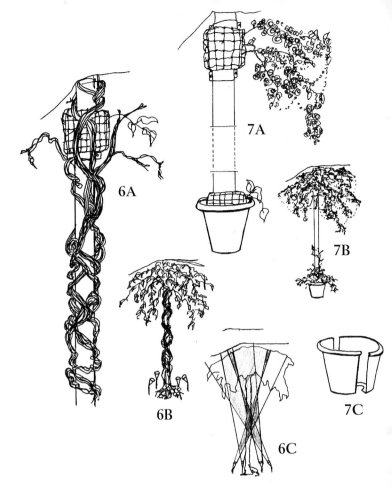

4A. *A wire hanging basket is suspended from a horizontal pole. Floral foam is kept secure with wire netting.*

4B. *This drawing shows a good height from the roof of the tent. This will need to be greater if candles are used as in the design shown in the photograph.*

5A. *A lovely idea for a Christmas wedding is an artificial or real Christmas tree suspended upside down from the marquee pole (if necessary two artificial trees could be used). Decorations and tree lights are added. Note how the garlands and baubles hang very much more attractively than when the tree is the right way up, as there are no lower branches to interfere with them.*

5B. *This drawing shows a very large tree, almost reaching the ground, but the effect is as attractive in any size.*

6A. *Twisted vine has been wound round and wired to the pole. A wire cage with foam is clamped at the top.*

6B. *The finished outline of the tree with the spot-lights in position. Trial and error will determine the best effect for the lighting.*

6C. *A simple outline drawing of light-beam directions. This idea could be used with many tree designs for evening decorations.*

It is sometimes impossible to place a marquee in the garden without having the problem of trees or shrubs which cannot be moved. Turn this to your advantage and add either flowers or lighting.

7A. *The basic mechanics again this time, using lovely blossom for a spring wedding. The base of the pole has been given a large pot to hold planted bulbs or ivies. Large, decorative stones look very attractive with the ivies, and moss looks very good with the bulbs.*

7B. *An outline sketch shows the finished design. The tiny decorative lights can be added to give a fairy-tale appearance.*

7C. *A detail to show the plastic flower-pot cut in half to put at the base of the pole. String or wire will hold the two pieces together and pot plants or foam and flowers can be used to decorate it if necessary.*

BUFFET TABLE DESIGN

1. *Lamp bases have been joined together with a central metal rod. Moulds have been set on to them and a candle cup has been screwed on to the top of the metal rod to take either a candle or extra flowers.*
2. *Foam and wire-netting mechanics.*
3. *The finished design for a winter wedding buffet. A lovely bow has been tied on to the base to add an extra festive feeling.*
(Alternative designs are shown on page 76.)

1   2   3

plan, but again, with some of the designs able to be made in advance, the actual arranging time needed will be negligible. The marquee is usually erected a day or so before the event, giving time for any last-minute changes in ideas that might be needed. It is important, though, to have finished the decor before the caterer moves in! The table arrangements can be left at one side on a spare table, to be placed in position by the catering staff when they are ready.

However, you must arrange the buffet table or cake table with the cloths on and in position (it is very simple to cover the table-cloth with plastic sheeting to avoid any spills); it is nigh on impossible to arrange flowers for these types of design and then move them later. The buffet and cake decor must be arranged in situ. A discussion with the caterer prior to arranging day will ensure that all goes according to plan.

The time schedule will be quite tight, especially if the flowers for the service have to be arranged. It therefore makes sense to create designs that can be easily worked and rely on drama and effect for the end result, rather than very pretty, finicky designs that could well be lost in such a large area. I am in no way suggesting simple or ordinary ideas are the order of the day – not at all – but I am saying that big and bold designs with good-sized materials are preferable. This is probably the most exciting and expensive party that you will ever have and it has to be super! Exotic, charming, frivolous, or what you will – only careful planning with attention to detail will ensure that the best possible use is made of the tent and the designs.

OPPOSITE *This elegant design has been arranged to make an attractive centrepiece for the buffet table. Frosted fruits and berries have been used to add a sparkle for a Christmas wedding. Artificial frosting should not be used where food is being served; egg white and caster sugar have been applied instead.*

As with the wedding service, plans and rough sketches will help to give a good feeling of the sizes needed. It is amazing how small an arrangement will seem when placed at the top of a marquee pole. Planning the decorations for a marquee is fun and only one step more enjoyable is actually doing them.

Themes

Country themes are a delight, with garden-type flowers such as marguerites and cow parsley, or sheaves of wheat and foliage garlands; or yet again an Italian theme, with decorated statuary and pillars; or a French theme of trees and topiary decorations, as though grown in pots *à la* Versailles. The ideas are endless, and so are the ways in which lighting can help to improve them.

Marquee Poles

The mechanics for the poles will probably present the greatest problem and each different idea will need a slightly different solution. Basically, a wire-netting cage with floral foam will answer many of the requirements, but these must be put up with clamps and not nailed, as is so often the case. The men who erect the marquees have to work very speedily, and even one nail that has not been removed properly can cause a nasty accident, or even, as one very sad worker told, badly torn canvas. Nailing up is easy but clamps are not so complicated and are much to be preferred. Wire-netting cages can be used in a number of ways and are very inexpensive. Alternatively, garlands can be made to twirl down and around the pole. If possible, it is a good idea to ask the marquee men to put a long piece of strong string over the bar, close to the pole, so that it will be a very simple exercise to hoist the

garland up as though it were a flag. Twisting it gently round the pole and securing it at the bottom will be simplicity itself. Hanging baskets are especially lovely for marquee flowers and can be planted or arranged baskets. Again, it is a good idea to ask the tent erecters to leave a strong string or wire over the top bar to allow the basket to be hoisted aloft.

OTHER BUFFET TABLE DESIGNS

1. *Wood and small branches have been worked to create the same tall style.*
2. *Glass dishes have been employed here to obtain the same height and slim design. A mock-marble base has been placed under the glass dishes to add even greater height and give some weight visually.*
3. *A plastic urn that has been painted to look like stone has a metal stand with three tiers to take the mechanics, which are taped very firmly into it.*

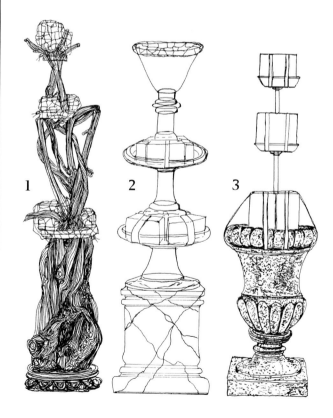

1   2   3

Viewing Levels

It is important to remember that the designs will be seen at ground level, and this is not always easy to visualize when working high up on a ladder. Rather than having to climb up and down to see how things are progressing, it is helpful to work with a partner who can hand up materials or give directions for placing flowers strategically . . . and also, of course, steady the steps! It is good to remind yourself that the designs will be seen from all angles and therefore an all-round design should be used.

If at all possible, try to see the marquee that is to be used at another venue, some time before the day that it will be needed (marquee hirers are very amenable), as this will help to iron out any wrinkles well ahead of A-day (Arranging Day).

Attention to Detail

One particular problem to be avoided is that of the too-short ladder. This happened to me on one occasion and the precarious balancing act that followed is not one I would recommend to anyone. Perhaps there is a tree or dovecot in the place where the marquee is to be sited; rather than fretting about the inconvenience, incorporate it into the designs.

Decorations for the poles can be worked in so many ways, and the choice must be suitable to the size and style. There are lovely ways to create the feeling of cascades of flowers tumbling from the roof, or tree ideas that can incorporate ribbons, fabrics, fruits, berries or tassels to make very special designs. These ideas are improved if they are linked with the decorations for the walls or the others being used in the tent.

The containers for a marquee must be stable; delicate stands and wobbly pedestals are not a good idea for grass, and even if there is matting,

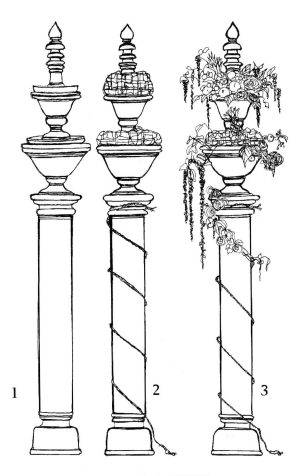

TALL DESIGNS FOR A MARQUEE BUFFET

1. *The tall pillar has been made from a drain pipe and then painted to look like terracotta (you could choose anything - stone, marble, whatever), with the addition of two urns. The urns have had moulds put in them to take the foam and then a 'top knot' of a decorative stairpost has been placed on a small support. Everything has been carefully assembled and held together with oasis fix. The urns, which were proper terracotta, were quite bright in colour, so they were softened with a dull brown and green emulsion to give a feeling of age.*
2. *Floral foam was cut to shape and placed in the moulds and then covered with wire netting, held in place with string. The line for a possible garland was marked.*
3. *The design was completed with fruits, flowers and vegetables in pinks and purples, with interesting materials such as Amaranthus to add another dimension to the design.*

The buffet table has been set with the tall designs in the background and matching urns on the table, creating a stunning effect for an evening party.

carpeting or flooring, these cannot be relied upon to provide a completely flat surface. Even a very heavy pedestal or a plastic one weighted with sand is not totally stable. One that has three legs gives a much better 'footing'!

The decorations in marquees are usually better if placed at a reasonable height or they will not be seen by many, if any, of the guests. Wall decorations are ideal as they require little space and certainly cannot be knocked over. Wall baskets and suggestions that can be used for pew ends are a good idea - on a larger scale, of course. Ribbon bows incorporated into the designs and trailing materials or stunning colour will help to accentuate the arrangements.

Statuary

One particular delight of mine when arranging flowers in a marquee is, if at all possible, to use statuary. It does not have to be the real thing; there are some very attractive plastic ideas and these look wonderful decorated with garlands or foliages. Some of the inexpensive bird-bath styles with a figure supporting a large dish look marvellous arranged with flowing designs, and are equally good used on a buffet table.

Table Designs

While tent designs need to be bold, and perhaps you need not be quite so fussy about perfect materials or the odd piece of floral foam showing, table decorations, on the other hand,

are viewed close to and will probably be studied in detail, so they must be flawless. Table designs must also be stable and arranged in such a way that the guests can see each other. With buffet table designs, it is important to ensure that they do not hinder the caterers in any way. Height is not important here, but tall, slim designs are preferable to wide, squat styles.

Small, inexpensive plastic dishes are very useful for table decorations. It is perfectly possible to use margarine pots or something similar, but do hide the name, if there is one, or paint it out! The plastic dishes will need just a small round or block of floral foam taped securely. These designs are always good for guests to take home and will certainly continue to be enjoyed for many days after the wedding. It is a great pity that so often they

The elegant and very simple designs used for the lunch table are easily arranged and give an uncluttered feeling to the decor. Easily made well ahead of time, the design can be later transferred to a side table as a buffet decoration. Glass must be smear-free and sparkling to give the best appearance.

The corsage, seen on the table, is a lovely idea for a spring wedding, either for a bride or her mother.

are simply thrown away after the reception; a little planning will ensure that this is not necessary.

Small arrangements in a plastic dish can be very dull, resembling a stodgy pudding rather than a delightfully arranged design. Trailing pieces of pretty foliage and attention to relative heights will avoid the 'pudding syndrome'. Small baskets are another good idea for table decorations and are easy to carry home afterwards. Floral foam rings are a great favourite of mine and are a delight, especially in spring, with all the pretty materials in delicate colourings. Table arrangements do need interesting materials and care with arrangement. It is so easy to try and dash them off at the end of arranging everything else that they are often worked on by tired arrangers, who just want to get home, or created from the pieces that have been left over from larger designs. By planning carefully, you can obviously save flowers and foliages from large heads of flowers that have been carefully thinned and from special foliages that have had excess pieces cut out of them. Never think that the left-over bits and pieces will be adequate; these designs are as important as any of the others.

Table arrangements should be sensibly sized for the space and allow the guests to view one another, without having to peer through a vast display of flowers and foliages. Arranging the designs sitting down will not only give your legs and feet a well-earned rest but also enable you to work at the angle from which they will be seen.

Buffet Tables

Buffet tables are usually a good area to decorate, but they must allow the caterers plenty of space to move about, so they can serve the food without hindrance. This is absolutely vital: I have seen an extremely irate caterer moving a very large arrangement out of the way, with disastrous results. Remember that each part of the ceremony is important and should complement the others for the best overall result. Stability, as I have mentioned, is also a consideration and if plastic urns are being used, it is preferable to use sand as the weighting element rather than water; the reason is not difficult to appreciate. Even if the container seems quite heavy with the wet floral foam and

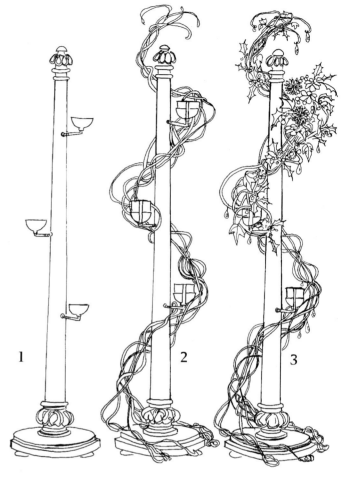

1 2 3

TALL POLE DESIGNS

Designs for limited space is important but all too frequently the solution is just narrow pedestals, which fail to be kept slim, get knocked about and generally interfere with movement. At any reception, space is always at a premium, especially in the entrance area, and a simple but striking design can help.
1. Wooden poles have been worked with holders which screw into the sides. These can be placed at will, although as the poles in this case are from an old cheval mirror, I do not often change the positions. There were some holes already there from when the mirror was attached, so it was not much of a problem.
2. The floral foam is placed in the cups and twisted vine is put around and through the design.
3. Holly and ivy with berries are added, with silk flowers for a Christmas wedding. A little glitter has been used and also one or two glass drops to sparkle in the candlelight, which will again match the lightly decorated dress of the bride.

The entrance to the winter wedding reception welcomes the guests with elegance and a suggestion of sparkle. The poles have been placed on either side of the doorway and the slim designs do not hinder guests as they enter.

flowers when these are being arranged, they will dry out considerably and become very unstable and so liable to topple over.

The Cake Table

The last, but certainly not the least, table that needs attention is that for the cake. Situations vary: sometimes the cake will be at the centre of the 'top table' and at others on a special dais and table of its own. Whichever, the cake area is special. I love to see a tiered cake sitting on a silver stand, set apart on a beautifully laundered table-cloth with elegant decorations. Many photographs will be taken of this particular area during the celebrations and it is well worth spending some time considering the best position and the type of decorations most suited to it.

Cake decorations are legion and to suggest arrangements that will cover them all is an impossibility. However, I have suggested some ideas which can be easily adapted. From a flower-arranging point of view, I do prefer real flower decorations on the cake and think that

THE CAKE TABLE

If a separate table is to be used for the wedding cake, it is important that it should look as lovely as possible. It will be a centre of attention and it is worth making an extra effort to provide the best setting for the cake, which is a very important part of the ceremony.

Although a card table is useful, despite the most elegant covering, it always seems to look just like a card table! Placing a chipboard roundel on the top or using a round table is much to be preferred. The simple mechanics that have been sketched show how a portable round table can be easily made and assembled. If a handy person can be persuaded to make one, ensure that they do not over-zealously glue it together; it is convenient to transport it in three flat pieces and then assemble it.

Covering the table is the next consideration. I always feel that at least three layers are good, and if possible use more. The underskirts do not need to be grand; they can be my special standby of old starched sheets. It does not matter if they are not level all the way round, as with several layers everything will work out perfectly. The final layer - and if finances allow, the second layer too - need to be properly made to fit the table. Expensive fabric is not always the most attractive. I have seen fine muslin beautifully gathered and well laundered look stunning. The secret is to have a full gathered skirt; a skimped one will look and feel mean, even in the most luxurious of materials.

the new idea of setting small tubes into the cake itself to take delicate arrangements is a delight. Here, you must liaise with the cake-maker, as the tubes have to be inserted before the cake is iced. The cake shown has been beautifully decorated with trailing designs which have then been echoed on the cloth.

Receptions cannot always be held at home these days and the number of alternatives available now is incredible - it really is true that almost anything goes! Cruisers, hotels, pubs, restaurants, boats, village halls, livery halls, barns, museums and stately homes are just a few of the many venues that can be used. The choice will be yours. Many of them will not allow you to decorate, but some will and certain of the designs shown can be happily adapted.

The time of year will also have some bearing on the choice of decorations. It is as important

OPPOSITE *Attaching garlands or swags to tables is easily managed if the uncovered table has a strong wire passed over and under it and then securely fastened in the position required. The tables are covered, the designs arranged in floral foam in flat trays (covered in fine film) and attached with safety pins through the cloths to the wires.*

to get out the notebook for the reception plans as it is for the wedding service designs. There could well be many more problems to solve, especially with a daytime affair becoming a disco for the younger element later. Chairs and tables will perhaps need two positions during the proceedings. It is better to plan beforehand than have to ask the best man to move the pedestal designs to allow the band to sit down!

The Receiving Line

If there is to be a receiving line, it is important that the decorations at this point are really special. The colour scheme should coordinate with the flowers used in the bridal bouquets if possible, or at least tone in with them. The guests waiting to be greeted will have ample time to study the designs in minute detail. Many photographs are taken at this point and a background of flowers is always a delight. A mantelpiece is a perfect position for such an arrangement if it is in the right position; if not, then an elegant pedestal design is also good. A particularly lovely area to decorate, if possible, is the staircase and banisters. Garlands are especially attractive here.

Village Hall Disguises

If using a village hall do not be overly concerned that it looks a little drab. By the time the decorations have been worked and the tables set with starched cloths and flowers, it will be super. If the hall really is a disaster area, it can be transformed with a lining of some kind, but usually this is unnecessary and the trick of placing the decorations in strategic positions will draw attention away from any eyesores.

Some hotels or halls will have splendid containers that you might be able to use (it is

BUFFET DESIGN

Simple and elegant designs for a winter wedding buffet table.
1. *Wooden pedestals placed closely together, with a candleholder on the taller of the two and a tray with floral foam and wire netting wired securely on the other. A string has been wound round the two as a guide for the garland of small fruits and berries.*
2. *The garland is carefully worked and a large candle placed in the holder.*
3. *The design is completed with a beautiful but contained arrangement.*

always worth asking). Not only will it save having to take your own pedestals and dishes to the hall, but they will probably be very beautiful and just right for the setting. It is good to arrange this when a preliminary visit is made. If there are no suitable containers, or perhaps none that you will be allowed to use, you will need to plan ahead for what will be needed. The containers should be suitable to the venue, of course, and some thought must be given to

The buffet table set in readiness for the guests for a winter wedding. The designs look very elegant in the wonderful setting but do not overpower the scene. All is in good proportion to allow each decorative feature a space to be at its very best.

transportation. Certainly plastic containers are light to move about, but they will look very out of place in a stately home next to the 'real thing'. If possible, choose simple wooden stands for such settings; they will settle into the surroundings much more comfortably.

Decorating the chosen venue is not always easy, especially if it is being used the day before the wedding and is not available until the morning. Table decorations can be worked ahead of time and taken on the day, and the arrangements planned well in advance to involve the minimum of work. Instead of garlands on the top table, smilax or ivies can be quickly placed there; garlands need quite some time to get them fixed correctly. Such labour-saving ideas will help greatly. This is certainly a time when all hands will be needed.

Planning Ahead

It is important to take with you any floral foam that is to be used, thoroughly soaked and then allowed to dry a little. Hotels and village halls do not usually have adequate facilities for soaking quantities of foam blocks in the cloakrooms and the kitchen staff will not be overly enthusiastic about you invading their domain. As long as it has been well soaked and then allowed to drain a little - but make sure it does not dry out completely - it will readily take up water again when in the container. If it seems a little reluctant to do so, a small amount of washing-up liquid in the water will work wonders.

Not only foam but all your mechanics will need to be prepared and checked as they are packed. There will be no time to rush out and buy more, even if there is a shop nearby! Foliages and flowers must all have been well conditioned; the reception venue will invariably be warmer than the church and flowers will not last well unless they are thoroughly prepared.

It is advisable to leave instructions with the manager, or whoever is in charge, as to when you will come back to clear up. This will really only be necessary if you have used your own containers or if it has been agreed that you will remove the flowers afterwards for the family to keep or perhaps to give to a nearby hospital. The hotel might be happy to keep the arrangements, but whatever the decision that is made, you should put it in writing so that everything is quite clear.

Honeymoon Plans

With honeymoons, it is often the case that the bride and groom will not leave until quite late in the day, or possibly even on the next day, and so there will be a choice of plans to be followed. I particularly like the old-fashioned way, with the young couple leaving after the wedding breakfast at a reasonable hour, giving everyone the joy of seeing them off and wishing them well. It is always so special to throw rose petals and rice as the car drives away, and particularly so for the one who catches the bouquet. It then leaves the guests to chat about the day and perhaps have a simple dinner party to talk about old times and old friends.

But new times have heralded new ideas for wedding celebrations: the evening party, be it a ball or a disco. For me, it bears no comparison to seeing the bride throwing her bouquet and then watching the car noisily disappearing into the distance, decorated this time not with flowers but with cans, streamers and old boots!

CHECKLIST

CHOICE OF VENUE:
HOME
HOTEL
VILLAGE HALL
GARDEN

DESIGNS FOR SPECIAL NEEDS
TENTS
MARQUEES
BUFFET TABLE
CAKE TABLE

8

ADAPTING AND CREATING ARRANGEMENTS FOR EVENING PARTIES

So MANY WEDDING RECEPTIONS are held in the evening or continue on from the afternoon celebrations that a word about the specific needs for these times is perhaps necessary. Certainly, if the hall or marquee has to be rearranged to accommodate a disco or suchlike, some of the flower designs will need to be thought about very carefully.

If the tables do not have to be altered, then it is good to create a slightly different atmosphere for the evening party. This can involve a simple exercise such as placing candles in holders of some kind, which can then be easily pushed into the flower arrangements on the tables.

Hanging baskets are a lovely way to decorate a marquee and as long as there is a really good space between the candles and the canvas roof (ensure that candles are well fixed into their holders), this will give a very attractive effect. Remember that a candle fixative is essential: unless they are completely safe, I would not risk using candles in this way. It is also important never to leave lit candles anywhere at anytime unattended. For lighting and extinguishing candles that are high up, the gadget used in churches for just such a purpose is useful.

Safety when using candles is essential. There are several very good ideas that are available in department stores. It is well worth investigating all the gadgets that are offered.

Lighting for Evening Parties

Christmas tree lights are another lovely idea to use with flowers, and especially with foliages and painted branches. The effect at night is beautiful, transforming the area into a twinkling delight. Lighting directed up into the ceiling or roof of a marquee is easily managed and looks particularly good under trees and tall trailing designs. I also love the idea of lighting under obelisks, giving them a striking and exciting appearance. Wire frames with foliages and flowers look wonderful lit from within the design; this is a good idea for porches and entrances.

Floodlights

Floodlighting is a marvellous way to transform the scene and flowers positively 'blossom' when it is right. But equally they can look awful in certain types of light and colourings. Orange or red lighting is a disaster, but soft peach or warm pink is just right. Remember that red and blue flowers will disappear in the dark and that it is the lighter shades, particularly creams, lemons and peaches, or those in the luminous group of colourings (tints are in this category – that is, colours to which white has been added), you need as they will be seen

A hanging basket is a very simple but attractive idea for a marquee decoration. A gardener could well create growing plants for such a design. Here floral foam has been used and very simple materials have been arranged to give a light and airy design.

more easily in dim or darker situations. If there is any doubt as to a choice of colourings for evening, it is worth consulting colour schemes and a colour wheel for help – not the one found in paint shops but the one used by flower arrangers. Good information on colour can be had from The National Association of Flower Arranging Societies. Many books on basic flower arranging will also have this information.

With all ideas for lighting, be it with candles or with electricity, safety is the key word. If there is any doubt as to wiring, get advice from an expert. All outdoor bulbs and wires should be carefully covered and a safety cut-out

CANDELABRUM

The candelabrum is growing designs of ivy plants, but can be worked equally well with floral foam and ivy trails.
1. Wire frame.
2. Wire frame set into pot with potting compost and planted with four ivy plants. (If time does not allow for the ivies to grow to their full height, then the pot can be filled with foam and long trails can be wound through and up the frame.)
3. During the growing time the plants will need to be trimmed and fed well. Add the candles and, if desired, ribbon bows. The ribbons look very attractive if they are either wired or stiffened to give a good shape. Wired ribbon can be purchased and the stiffener can be papier-mâché or a special stiffening agent.

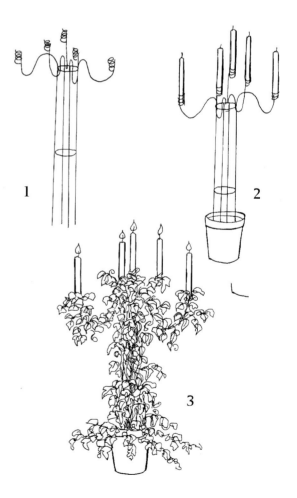

AN ALTERNATIVE CANDELABRUM

This can be set into the neck of a champagne bottle (it has to be a magnum to obtain a good fit). A lovely idea that can be used for many occasions.
1. Place a mould over the neck of the magnum.
2. Weight the bottle with sand or water. Cut floral foam to shape and place in the mould and tape well to keep secure.
3. Decorate with flowers, berries and foliages and insert the candleholder. Fit the candles securely into the holders, using a fixative if necessary.

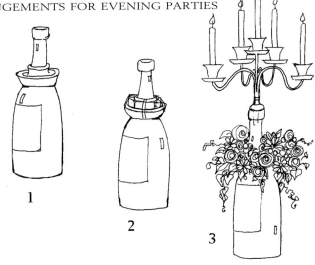

switch on the extension lead is essential. Many garden lights have a transformer, which is a very good idea.

Candlelight

The tall candle stands used in the aisle in a church design are useful for lighting terraces and pathways to the marquee and are very stable. If they are to be used on grass, I think it sensible to anchor them down with metal tent pegs to prevent any problems. The small night-lights are safely housed in glass shades. Night-lights are very useful for inexpensive decorating and look pretty if placed on small mirrors; this not only looks attractive but also gives more light. The table decorations shown in the marquee are suitable for night-lights and look delightful when used in this way.

The candelabra shown are a lovely way to use candles and give a good light. They are very stable and simple in design. Ribbon bows or other decorations can be added to give colour and interest, although I feel that they are sufficiently good to leave as they are.

If dancing of some kind is planned, I do think that a special area should be allocated. If necessary, move tall flower designs and any of those with candles well away. Nobody wants an accident to mar the day, and sometimes over-enthusiastic dancers do tend to get carried away (and why not). Taking precautions to avoid any problems is obviously the sensible thing to do.

The celebrations will probably last well into the night, if not well into the morning! All will be delightful, a night to remember with pleasure, perhaps ending with a firework display lighting up happy faces and the flowers in the garden.

CHECKLIST

DESIGNS THAT ARE READILY ADAPTABLE

LIGHTING

9

AFTER THE WEDDING

THE CELEBRATIONS are now memories; the photographs, the films and the videos will replay the events. But until the clearing away is completed, all is not quite over. It is a little sobering to have to get down to the unenviable job of removing the decorations, but the marquee men or the caterers will arrive promptly and everything will have to be ready for them.

It is more than probable that the flowers for the service will be left for the congregation to enjoy. They can be removed at a later date, but it is usual to remove the pew end and lych gate decorations, if any were arranged. Pillar decorations are usually allowed to remain with the other designs. Perhaps the flowers that were arranged on the altar might have to be moved, to allow services to take place.

Reusing Flowers from the Wedding

All the flowers might have to be removed - for example, if the vicar allowed flowers for a wedding in Lent, on the understanding that they

IVY TREE

The ivy tree decoration is one that can be grown or made with floral foam. Time will of course determine which course you take.
1. A broom handle is set into a cement base and dried ivy stems are twisted around the handle and wired in position.
2. A block of floral foam is set on to the top of the broom handle, covered with wire netting and wired very firmly in place. The cement base is set into a basket with floral foam, and wire netting is placed over and secured firmly. Long ivy trails are wound from top to bottom, pushing both ends of the stem into the foam.
3. The base is covered with grasses or moss and the top of the 'tree' is finished with ivy arranged as though growing. An alternative is to replace the foam with plants of ivy well bound together with garden twine and wired to the top of the broom handle. Plants are also placed in the basket at the base. Time and a little trimming and feeding will bring good results.
A ribbon string bow also looks attractive.

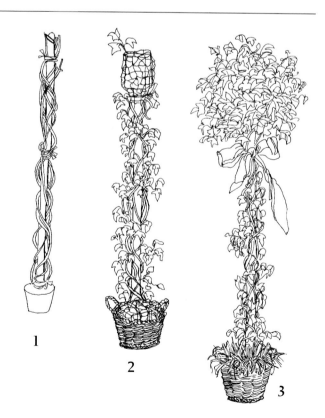

1

2

3

were removed afterwards. If this is the case, it is a lovely idea to take as many as possible to a hospital or old folks` home for them to enjoy. I know that hospitals are not thrilled with flowers from funerals and, as busy places, certainly do not want lots of materials that need to be arranged. Ready-made decorations of wedding flowers, though, are usually very well received, although it is wise to check first that they will be welcome. Hospices are especially good places to offer flowers.

Clearing away is not the best of jobs, but it is essential. Now is the time for all hands to be on deck. There are always a few stalwarts who turn up to help, and they are worth their weight in gold, but it is a good idea to plan the clearing-up team just as you did for the arranging team – both are important. With lots of helpers, everything seems to be cleared away in a trice; wth two or three, it takes for ever.

Retrieving Mechanics

A list of mechanics to be rescued is a good idea. In the rush to get finished, pinholders and treasured wire netting can very easily disappear with the rubbish. Large black rubbish sacks are a boon and can be painlessly and cleanly disposed of on a rubbish heap or, if there is a great deal, at the local tip. Nobody minds taking a bag or two of rubbish away if it is tidily put into a clean plastic sack, but enthusiasm can wear a little thin if people are asked to take dead materials just shoved into the boot of the car (even if they are in a flower box).

Cleaning tools will be needed, such as a dustpan and brush, a long-handled brush and mopping-up cloths or dusters. A vacuum cleaner is often to be found in the vestry, but do not use it for thick sticks or wet soggy leaves; they will clog it up very quickly! It is better to sweep up the materials first and then vacuum if necessary afterwards. Obviously a

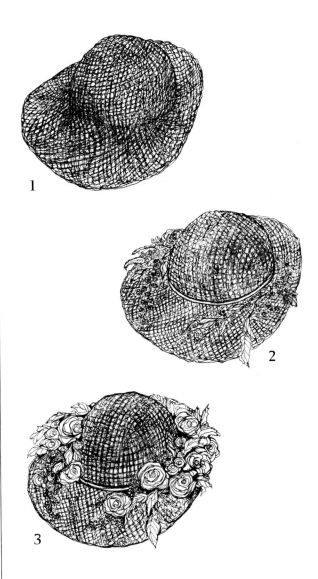

DECORATED HAT

A simple basic hat can become a sensation when beautifully decorated.
1. Basic hat.
2. Fine ribbon stitched on to hat. Simple wired flowers are placed roughly to assess the appearance.
3. The flowers are wired as for a headdress and stitched on to the hat carefully with matching thread.

hotel will not expect you to do a marathon clean-up, but it is reasonable to take your rubbish and leave things as tidy as possible. Yes, this applies to all the venues, even the garden.

Returning Borrowed Containers

Any containers that have been borrowed should be returned promptly. Otherwise they will disappear into the back of the garage and you will have a friend vowing never to lend

OPPOSITE *The ivy tree shown is one that I have grown and it is a delight on many occasions. Here it is a decoration for an entrance to the house, where the bride has left her hat on a chair.*

you another thing. It is only right to return containers clean and tidy, not still harbouring tatty foam, old wire netting or rotting foliages.

When all is cleared away, take a good look round to ensure that everything is as it should be. If you had one, return the key. It is good to check carefully that nothing has been left behind at this stage; you don`t want to have to return at a later date to pick up a cardigan or flower bucket!

Everything will look very clean and rather bare after the decorations have been removed, and sometimes I feel that it looks a little sad. However, all is in readiness for the next wedding flower decorations. You will leave with the happiest memories of a very, very beautiful day.

CHECKLIST

LIST OF ITEMS TO BE RETURNED

PROMPT ACTION

INDEX OF FLOWERS AND FOLIAGES

THE FOLLOWING list is a selection of flowers and foliages that I enjoy using and thoroughly recommend. If any special conditioning is required it has been included, with a code for easy identification. It must be remembered, however, that for satisfactory results all plant materials should have some conditioning care before being arranged. No grey-leaved foliage should be submerged in water.

Key to conditioning code
A   Boil or burn stem ends and give cool drink in deep water.
B   Crush stem ends and give warm drink in deep water.
C   Submerge in water.

Acanthus   A
Alchemilla mollis (ladies' mantle)
Alstroemeria (Peruvian lily)
Althaea (hollyhock)
Amaranthus caudatus viridis (green love-
    lies-bleeding)   A
Anemone × *hybrida* (windflower)
Anthriscus sylvestris (cow parsley, Queen
    Anne's Lace)   A
Antirrhinum
Aquilegia
Arum italicum 'Pictum'   C
Arum lily (*Zantedeschia*)
Asparagus asparagoides (smilax)
Aspidistra

Aster (Michaelmas daisy/'September flower')
Astrantia major
Atriplex hortensis alba and *h*. 'Rubra'
Aucuba japonica (spotted laurel)
Azalea   B

Beech (*Fagus sylvatica*)   B
Bouvardia
Bergenia cordifolia (pig squeak)

Cabbage (ornamental)
Campanula (Canterbury bell)
Cardoon (*Cynara cardunculus*. Similar to
    artichoke, but hardier for decoration)   A
Catkins (*Salix* and *Corylus*)   B
Choisya ternata (Mexican orange)   B
Chrysanthemum
Clematis   A
Clematis vitalba (old man's beard)
Cobaea scandens
Convallaria (lily-of-the-valley)
Cornflowers (*Centaurea cyanus*)
Corylus (hazel)   B
Cow parsley (*Anthriscus sylvestris*)   A

Dahlia
Delphinium
Dianthus (carnations)
Dicentra spectabilis (especially the white
    variety)   A
Dictamnus albus
Digitalis (foxglove: I love the white and
    apricot ones)

Eleagnus ebbingei ('Limelight' is a good
    variety for decorations)   B

Eucalyptus
Euphorbia (spurge)   A
Eustoma   A
Exochorda

Fagus sylvatica (beech)   B
Fatsia
Ferns (bracken, *Adiantum*, *Athyrium* and
   Osmunda)   A
Forsythia   B

Garrya elliptica
Guelder rose (*Viburnum opulus* 'Sterile')   B
Gladiolus (gladioli)

Hazel (*Corylus*)   B
Heather
Hedera (ivy)   C
Hellebore   A
Heracleum (hogweed)
Heuchera   A
Hosta
Hyacinth
Hydrangea   A

Jasmine (*Jasminum officinale*/summer
   flowering)

Larkspur
Lathyrus latifolius (**perennial sweet pea**)
Laurus (laurel)
Ligustrum (privet)
Lilium (lily)
Lily-of-the-valley (*Convallaria*)
Lime   B
Lonicera (honeysuckle)
Lupinus (lupin)

Matthiola (stock)
Moluccella (bells of Ireland)
Myrtus (myrtle)

Narcissus
Neillia   B
Nicotiana (tobacco plant)
Nigella (love-in-a-mist)

Pachysandra terminalis
Paeonia (peony)

Papaver (poppy)
Philadelphus (mock orange)
Physocarpus opulifolius aureus   B
Pittosporum (although *Rhamnus* is my
   preference, if available)
Polygonatum (Solomon's seal)
Prunus (flowering cherry, almond etc., and
   P. lusitanica)
Pyrus communis

Ranunculus
Rhus (smoke bush)
Ribes (flowering currant)   B
Rosa (rose)   A
Rubus tricolor and *R.* 'Benenden', syn.
   R. 'Tridel'.
Ruscus

Salix (catkin bearers)
Scabiosa caucasica (scabious)
Sedum
Senecio
Smilax (*Asparagus asparagoides*)
Snowball tree (*Viburnum opulus* 'Sterile')   B
Snowberry (*Symphoricarpos*)
Solidago (golden rod)
Solomon's seal (*Polygonatum*)
Sorbus aria (whitebeam)   B
Stephanandra
Symphoricarpos (snowberry)
Syringa (lilac)   B

Tuberose
Tulipa (tulip)

Viburnum opulus 'Sterile' and *V. tinus*   B
Vinca

Whitebeam (*Sorbus aria*)   B

Zinnia var. 'Envy'

Where I have added the botanical names it has
been to help with the choice of variety. The
florist will not always be familiar with the correct name for certain flowers and will, for
example, sell asters (Michaelmas daisies) as
'September flower', which is not to be found in
a garden plant guide.

GENERAL INDEX